D0505413

ESSENTIAL
RIO DE JANEIRO

★ Best places to see 34–55

■ Featured sight

■ Centro and São Cristóvão 79–92

■ Copacabana and Urca 113–124

■ Santa Teresa and Lapa 93–102

■ Lagoa 125–134

■ Guanabara Bay to Tijuca Forest
103–112

■ Ipanema 135–151

Written by Jane Egginton

© AA Media Limited 2012
ISBN: 978-0-7495-7164-1

Published by AA Publishing, a trading name of AA Media Limited, whose registered
office is Fanum House, Basing View, Basingstoke, Hampshire RG21 4EA. Registered
number 06112600.

AA Media Limited retains the copyright in the original edition © 2012 and in all
subsequent editions, reprints and amendments

A CIP catalogue record for this book is available from the British Library

A ... be used for private and personal use. This book or
any part of it may not be reproduced or stored by any means or in any form. Inquiries
re... to any uses of this book should be directed to the Publisher.

The content of this book is believed to be accurate at the time of printing. Due to
its ... likely to vary or change and the publisher is not responsible
for ... responsible for the consequences of any
re... rights that are given
to consumers under applicable law is not affected. Opinions expressed are for
guidance ... based on their experience at the time
of review and may differ from the reader's opinions based on their subsequent
experience.

We have tried to ensure accuracy in this guide, but things do change, so please let us
know if you have any comments at travelguides@theAA.com.

Colour separation: AA Digital Department
Printed and bound in Italy by Printer Trento S.r.l.

Find out more about AA Publishing and the wide range of services the AA provides
by visiting our website at theAA.com/shop

A03998
Mapping in this title produced from map data supplied by Global Mapping,
Brackley, UK. Copyright © Global Mapping/ITMB
Transport maps © Communicarta Ltd, UK

About this book

This book is divided into six sections.

The essence of Rio de Janeiro 6–19
Introduction; Features; Food and drink; Essential experiences

Planning 20–33
Before you go; Getting there; Getting around; Being there

Best places to see 34–55
The unmissable highlights of any visit to Rio de Janeiro

Best things to do 56–75
Beautiful beaches; stunning views; places to take the children and more

Exploring 76–151
The best places to visit in Rio de Janeiro, organized by area

Excursions 152–182
Places to visit out of town

Maps
All map references are to the maps on the covers. For example, Pão de Açúcar has the reference ➕ 24G – indicating the grid square in which it is to be found

Admission prices
Inexpensive (under R$10)
Moderate (R$10–R$25)
Expensive (over R$25)

Hotel prices
Prices are per room per night:
$ budget (under R$300)
$$ moderate (R$300–R$600)
$$$ expensive (over $600)

Restaurant prices
Prices are for a three-course meal per person without drinks:
$ budget (under R$60)
$$ moderate (R$60–R$100)
$$$ expensive (over R$100)

Contents

THE ESSENCE OF...

6 – 19

PLANNING

20 – 33

BEST PLACES TO SEE

34 – 55

BEST THINGS TO DO

EXPLORING...

EXCURSIONS

56 – 75   76 – 151   152 – 182

The essence of...

Introduction   8–9

Features   10–11

Food and drink   12–15

Essential experiences   16–19

Perched on top of Rio's green hills are the outstretched arms of Cristo Redentor (Christ the Redeemer) and the swinging cable car at Pão de Açúcar (Sugarloaf Mountain) – icons that have made this city famous throughout the world. The historic centre is dotted with colonial churches, museums and cultural centres, while beyond, Rio state offers getaways of all descriptions. For many, though, the true heart of Rio is in the famous twin beaches of Copacabana and Ipanema, and in the locals known as Cariocas, who make any visit here a delight.

features

ON THE BEACH

Rio is blessed with beautiful beaches and its population makes full use of them. On any day of the year, locals can be seen on the sand, sunbathing and playing volleyball, but also holding forth in pensioners' clubs, managing crèches and even taking business meetings.

BOTEQUIMS AND BOTECOS

Equally treasured are Rio's neighbourhood table-service bars, known as *botequims*, originally corner shops, bars, restaurants and even post offices. The even smaller and often shabby *botecos*, usually nothing more than a hole in the wall with a little standing room, are sometimes known as *pé-sujo*, or "dirty foot" bars.

CARNAVAL

Rio's Carnaval is unabashed *fantasia* (fantasy). *Escolas de Samba* (Samba Schools) sing, dance and beat their drums, parading in front of a panel of judges and 50,000 spectators

in the purpose-built Sambódromo stadium. Elsewhere, *blocos* (groups of people) perform themed costume events in different neighbourhoods – one of the most well known is Banda de Ipanema, with its drag queens – and there are street festivities and masquerade balls.

SAMBA

African rhythms remembered by slaves in the northeast of Brazil made their way south, where in the *botequims* and homes of Rio, samba was born. Although its heyday was the 1920s, it remains the classic soundtrack to this exotic city. The lifeblood of Carnaval, samba can be heard in the traditional *gafieiras* (dance halls) of Lapa, in Centro's cultural centres, in the city's streets and bars, and even on its beaches.

COLONIAL HISTORY

Rio's historical heart is Centro, where most of its colonial buildings are found. The city became the capital of the Portuguese colony in 1775, and a quarter of a century later, with Napoleon snapping at its heels, the royal family fled Portugal and set up court here. As the new seat of the kingdom, Rio leapt in stature, attracting increased investment in infrastructure, architecture, the arts and sciences.

LANDSCAPE

The sweeping Atlantic beaches are one part of Rio's extraordinary physical beauty. Strung out along the coast are steep green *morros* (hills), covered in huge swathes of Atlantic rainforest, while lying low in the middle of the city is a vast saltwater lake. Rio's well-kept city parks contrast with the hillside *favelas* (shanty towns), and the 20th-century building boom has left many a neighbourhood with uninspiring buildings. But the bigger picture is a mesmerizing one – of a city carved from the jungle, at one with the ocean.

food & drink

Rio's cuisine is a reflection of its diverse population, which is made up of descendants of the original native Indian population, Portuguese settlers and African slaves, as well as German, Italian, Spanish, Arab and Japanese migrants. The collective influences of this eclectic mix, and the availability of a wide variety of ingredients across the country, have given birth to some unique cooking styles that can be found throughout the city.

RICE AND BEANS

Feijão com arroz (rice and beans) is a Brazilian staple and can be found everywhere. *Feijoada*, a slowly simmered stew of black or red beans with pork, is the national dish, served with orange slices, toasted manioc flour, collard greens and rice in Rio's restaurants, traditionally for a leisurely Saturday lunch.

EUROPEAN CUISINE

In Rio de Janeiro, pizza is as popular as any Brazilian dish, sold in sophisticated Italian restaurants as well as in snack bars. The Portuguese influence is seen in *bolos* (cakes) and in dried salted codfish balls, *bacalhau*, a popular bar snack that is surprisingly delicious.

SPICY STEWS AND SNACKS

Many of the dishes that evolved from the African slave plantations in Bahia in the northeast of Brazil can be found across Rio. The heart of many Bahian meals is the holy trinity of coconut, malagueta pepper and dendê oil (made from the fruit of a palm tree brought to Brazil by African slaves). Restaurants in Rio offer steaming vats of Bahian stews like *ximxim de galinha*, made with chicken and shrimp, or fish stew, known as

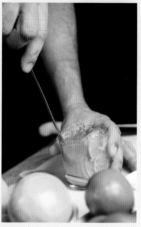

moqueca baiana, and casual street stands in local markets hawk Bahian spicy bean snacks known as *acarajé*.

MEAT ON THE MENU

All over Rio are *churrascarias* (barbecue restaurants), serving, delicious and tender sizzling meat. At *rodizos* (all-you-can-eat restaurants), diners can feast on as much meat as well as salads and sushi as they wish for a fixed price.

DRINKING RIO STYLE

Do what the locals do. Have a *cafezinho* (little coffee) at a neighbourhood bar or coffee shop to kick start your day, a refreshing *água de coco* (coconut water) to rehydrate yourself at the beach, and finish up with a cool *chopp* (draught beer) or two at sunset. Juice bars are found on almost every street corner, selling a huge range of delicious fresh *sucos* (juices) of almost every kind you can imagine, as well as those made from exotic Amazonian fruits such *açai* and *guaraná*.

THE SPIRIT OF BRAZIL

Brazil's most popular spirit is *cachaça*, distilled from fermented sugar cane. It is made all over the country and sometimes aged in barrels to give a smoother finish. *Cachaça* is commonly used in cocktails, including the delicious and potent national drink, *caipirinha*, where it is muddled with sugar, lime, ice and *batida*, a combination of condensed milk and fruit.

essential experiences

If you only have a short time to visit Rio and would like to take home some unforgettable memories, the following suggestions will give you a wide range of sights and experiences that won't take very long, won't cost very much and will make your visit a very special one.

● **Admire the art** at one of the changing exhibitions at the thriving cultural centre, Centro Cultural Banco do Brasil (➤ 92).

● **Watch a football** match and cheer with the crowds at the legendary Maracanã stadium (➤ 38–39).

● **Shake to samba** with live music at the Rio Scenarium bar and club (➤ 102).

● **Fly like a bird** as you hang-glide down from the hill of São Conrado before landing on the beach (➤ 145).

● **Feast on barbecued meat** at a traditional *churrascaria* (➤ 14).

● **Take to the hills** and hike through the

vast wilderness of
Parque Nacional da
Tijuca (➤ 46–47).

● **Visit Rio's most
famous icon**, the
Cristo Redentor statue
(➤ 36–37) and enjoy
its sweeping views of
the city.

● **Relax on the beach**
with the beautiful
people in Ipanema
(➤ 52–53).

● **Take the historic tram** to bohemian Santa Teresa (► 96–97), with its delightful neighbourhood restaurants and boutiques.

● **Ride the cable car** up to Pão de Açúcar (Sugarloaf; ► 44–45), James Bond-style.

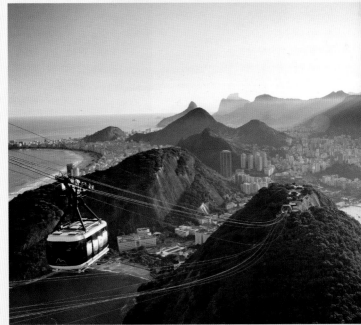

Planning

Before you go   22–25

Getting there   26–27

Getting around   28–29

Being there   29–33

Before you go

WHEN TO GO

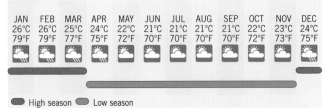

JAN	FEB	MAR	APR	MAY	JUN	JUL	AUG	SEP	OCT	NOV	DEC
26°C	26°C	25°C	24°C	22°C	21°C	21°C	21°C	21°C	22°C	23°C	24°C
79°F	79°F	77°F	75°F	72°F	70°F	70°F	70°F	70°F	72°F	73°F	75°F

🔵 High season 🔵 Low season

There isn't a best or worst time to visit Rio. In summer (December to February), the city is buzzing, the beach takes the edge off the heat and humidity, and a fast, furious downpour to clear the air is never far away. During this time, flights and accommodation become more expensive. From April until September, the air is cooler, the beach is quieter and prices drop (a little). From then, the atmosphere builds again as the Brazilians get back in the mood for summer and, of course Carnaval (February or March). Visit then and your reward is the excitement of the world's greatest party, though it won't come cheap – be prepared for huge price hikes and book as early as you can.

WHAT YOU NEED

		UK	Germany	USA	Netherlands	Spain
● Required	Some countries require a passport to remain valid for a minimum period (usually at least six months) beyond the date of entry – contact their consulate or embassy or your travel agent for details.					
○ Suggested						
▲ Not required						
Passport		●	●	●	●	●
Visa (regulations can change – check before you travel)		▲	▲	●	▲	▲
Onward or Return Ticket		○	○	○	○	○
Health Inoculations (polio)		○	○	○	○	○
Health Documentation (► 23, Travel and Health Insurance)		▲	▲	▲	▲	▲
Travel Insurance		○	○	○	○	○
Driving Licence (national or international)		●	●	●	●	●
Car Insurance Certificate (provided by car rental company)		●	●	●	●	●
Car Registration Document (provided by car rental company)		●	●	●	●	●

WEBSITES

- The Brazilian Tourist Office
www.braziltour.com
- Official Rio Guide
www.rioguiaoficial.com.br
- Insider's Guide to Rio
www.ipanema.com
- State Tourist Office
www.turisrio.rj.gov.br

TOURIST OFFICES AT HOME

In the UK
✉ 32 Green Street
London W1K 7AT
☎ +44 20 7399 9000
www.brazil.org.uk
In the USA
✉ 3006 Massachusetts Avenue,
NW Washington, DC
20008-3634
☎ +1 202/238-2805
www.brasilemb.org

In Canada
Brazilian Embassy
✉ 450 Wilbrod Street
Ottawa, Ontario
K1N 6M8
☎ +1 613/237-1090
www.brasembottawa.org
In Germany
☎ +49 69 9623 8733
In Spain
☎ +34 91 503 0687

TRAVEL AND HEALTH INSURANCE

Check your travel insurance includes a minimum of £2 million towards medical treatment. If you go abroad more than twice a year, an annual policy should be better value than single-trip insurance. Look for couple and family deals too. Emergency dental treatment is expensive – check it's covered by your medical insurance. Keep bills for insurance claims.

TIME DIFFERENCES

| GMT 12 noon | Rio de Janeiro 8AM | Germany 1PM | USA (NY) 7AM | Netherlands 1PM | Spain 1PM |

In winter, Rio is 4 hours behind London. Come summer, clocks in Rio go forward an hour and English clocks go back an hour, so Rio is just 2 hours behind London.

Similarly, Rio is 1 hour ahead of New York, stretching to 3 hours in the summer.

WHAT'S ON WHEN

January *Festa de São Sebastião* Religious and music festivities throughout the city honour Rio's patron saint (20 January).

February/March *Carnaval* For the five days before Ash Wednesday there are explosive events in the Sambódromo stadium and in the streets of Rio.

March/April *Semana Santa* (Holy Week) Religious processions and events throughout the city, beginning on Good Friday.

May–June *Rio das Ostras* (Jazz and Blues Festival) A five-day event, 170km (106 miles) east of Rio that attracts 20,000 people daily (end May–beginning June; www.riodasostrasjazzeblues.com).

June *Festas Juninas* Festivities with music, fireworks and food throughout the month, honouring the feast days of important saints. *Rio de Janeiro Marathon* A 42km (26-mile) coastal run from Recreio to Aterro do Flamengo (end June; www. maratonadorio.com.br).

June–July *Cinesul* A festival of Latin American, Spanish and Portuguese cinema and video (end June– beginning July; www.cinesul.com.br).

July *Anima Mundi* A 10-day international animation festival, held in various venues throughout the city (end July; www. animamundi.com.br).

August *Grand Prix* A horse race that takes place over three days at the Jockey Club (Jóquei Clube Brasileiro) in Gávea (first Sunday in August).

September *Dia da Independência do Brasil* Brazilian Independence Day celebrates the independence from Portugal in 1822 with a large military parade in Centro, and other processions throughout the city (7 September).
Bienal do Livro Rio The city's International Book Fair, taking place over 11 days every odd-numbered year, is one of Brazil's most important literary events, and includes readings and workshops (mid-September; www.bienaldolivro.com.br).

September/October *Festival do Rio* One of Latin America's largest film festivals, with screenings held throughout the city (end September–beginning October; www.visualnethost2.com.br/festrio).

October/November *Parada do Orgulho LGBT* A LGBT (lesbian/gay/bisexual/transvestite) parade that runs the length of Copacabana beach (dates vary; www.gaypridebrazil.org/rio-de-janeiro).

December *Iemanjá* During the festival of the Goddess of the Sea on New Year's Eve, religious offerings are made on the beaches of Copacabana and Ipanema.
Reveillon To bring in the New Year, *Iemanjá* (see above) culminates in a big party with sepctacular firework displays and live music on Copacabana beach.

NATIONAL HOLIDAYS

1 January *New Year's Day*
February/March *Carnaval*: five days before Ash Wednesday
Friday before Easter Sunday *Good Friday*
21 April *Tiradentes Day*
1 May *Labour Day*

62 days after Good Friday *Corpus Christi*
7 September *Independence Day*
21 October *Our Lady of Aperecida* (Patron Saint of Brazil)
2 November *All Souls' Day*
15 November *Republic Day*
25 December *Christmas Day*

Getting there

BY AIR

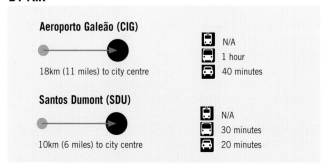

Aeroporto Galeão (CIG)

18km (11 miles) to city centre

N/A
1 hour
40 minutes

Santos Dumont (SDU)

10km (6 miles) to city centre

N/A
30 minutes
20 minutes

The vast majority of visitors to Rio arrive on an international flight, into Rio de Janeiro's Aeroporto Galeão (GIG). Many of these flights stop first at Aeroporto Guarulhos (GRU) in São Paulo, where through passengers remain on the aircraft, adding at least 90 minutes to the flight time. Rio's domestic airport is Santos Dumont (SDU), close to the historic centre of Rio.

AIRLINES
- The major airlines flying between Europe and Brazil are Air France, American Airlines, British Airways, Iberia, KLM, TAM and TAP. There are direct flights to Rio from London, Frankfurt, Madrid and Lisbon. Several other European capitals operate flights that briefly stop in São Paulo.
- Continental Airlines, Delta, United, US Airways and TAM fly from the USA. There are direct flights from Miami, Charlotte, Atlanta and Houston.
- Air Canada, Continental Airlines, TAM and United operate flights from Canada.
- Flights coming from Australia will typically require a stopover in Chile or Argentina. Aerolineas Argentina, Quantas/TAM and LAN are good options to consider.

FLIGHT TIMES

The flight time from Europe to Rio is between 10 and 14 hours, from the USA between 9 and 14, from Canada around 14 hours, and from Australia between 18 and 21.

GETTING FROM THE AIRPORT INTO THE CITY

- "Real" air-conditioned bus number 218 runs from the airport with drop-offs at Copacabana and Ipanema and terminates at Barra da Tijuca. The service operates roughly every half hour daily between 5:30am and 11pm. The journey, which costs R$7, takes at least an hour to Ipanema, but is often longer. Bear in mind that you will usually have to walk to your hotel or apartment from the bus stop – unless you take a cab.

- Local buses from the airport are even cheaper than the "Real", but are not recommended, as they are usually crowded, take even longer as they have more stops, and have no real space for luggage. There is no metro service from the airport.

- If you decide to take a taxi, you have two choices. You can buy a pre-paid ticket at one of the booths as you leave customs. At around R$80 for a fare to Ipanema, these taxis are the most expensive option, although at least you know the price is fixed and the cars are generally in better condition. Alternatively, take a yellow taxi from outside the terminal building. The drivers, or their touts, will try their best to overcharge you unless you bargain hard. The price to Ipanema with one of these taxis should be around R$50. You can also try to get the driver to agree to use the meter, although if you get stuck in heavy traffic, or the driver takes you the long way round, the price can significantly increase.

BY SEA

Cruise ships dock at the basic terminal facility at Pier Mauá, which is a 20-minute taxi ride to Ipanema, and just 10 minutes from the historic centre.

Getting around

PUBLIC TRANSPORT

Metro Rio's underground metro (Metrô Rio) is quick and safe, though its coverage of the city is limited. For visitors, the more useful of the two lines runs from the edge of Ipanema, into Copacabana, through Botafogo and Flamengo, to the historic centre and business district. The other line connects the centre to the north of the city via the Maracanã stadium. Single-journey tickets *(Unitário)* are fairly cheap, but for longer, more complex journeys, consider the better-value *Duplo*, which will cover interchanges onto buses.

Buses Buses are ubiquitous, although drivers can be erratic, and heavy traffic often makes journey times very slow. A conductor takes fares and operates the turnstile entry system, which helps to ensure safety, although buses are best avoided late at night. You can also buy tickets at metro stations that will cover your bus journey.

TAXIS

Most visitors will get to know Rio's taxis very well, hopping between bars and restaurants and beach districts. Particularly in the evening, when traffic is lighter and the streets are less crowded with people, a taxi ride makes more sense than walking or trying to negotiate public transport. Make sure the driver understands where you want to go, always insist that the meter is reset when you enter, and ask if it is working before you set off. Taxis can also be booked by telephone. Most drivers are friendly and more than helpful, and while most locals don't tip, drivers will appreciate it if you at least round up the fare to the nearest *real*. Consider hiring a taxi driver (ideally one you already know and trust) for a few hours or a day, including waiting time, for a fixed rate.

DRIVING

- Drive on the right side of the road.
- The speed limit is 80kph (50mph) in most towns and cities, and 110kph (70mph) on motorways.
- Seat belts are compulsory.

- Never drive under the influence of alcohol.
- Fuel prices vary greatly, even from day to day, but are generally lower than Europe and the US. Many petrol stations are dual fuel. When filling up, look for "A" for alcohol (ethanol) and "G" for gas (petrol).
- There is no national or city breakdown service, so it is a good idea to have a mobile phone with you.
- Car rental is relatively expensive. Most companies will not hire to anyone under the age of 21.

CYCLING

On Sundays, some of Rio's beachfront roads are closed to cars for parts of the day. Hiring a bicycle on those days is a pleasant way to get around. Cycling around the lake is also popular and there are a few miles of cycle paths in the Tijuca National Park.

Being there

TOURIST OFFICES
Aeroporto Galeão (CIG)
T1 International Arrivals, Blue Area
☎ (21) 3398 4077
🕓 Daily 6am–11pm
T1 Domestic Arrivals, Green Area
☎ (21) 3398 3034
🕓 Daily 7am–11pm
T2 International Arrivals
☎ (21) 3398 2245
🕓 Daily 6am–11pm
T2 Domestic Arrivals
☎ (21) 3398 2246
🕓 Daily 6am–11pm

Centro
Rua da Assembléia 10,
☎ (21) 2217 7575
🕓 Mon–Fri 9am–6pm
Copacabana
Avenida Princesa Isabel 183
☎ (21) 2541 7522
🕓 Mon–Fri 9–6
Beach Kiosk
Posto 6, Avenida Rainha Elizabeth
☎ (21) 2513 0077
🕓 Mon–Fri 9–5
Beach Kiosk
Posto 3–4, Rua Hilário de Gouveia
🕓 Daily 8am–10pm

Riotur (www.rioguiaoficial.com.br), Rio's official tourist agency, runs the above offices and kiosks, where English is spoken.

MONEY

The currency in Brazil is the *real* (BRL; R$). Notes are in denominations of 100, 50, 10, 5, 2 and 1 *real*, with coins of R$1, together with 50, 25, 10, 5 and 1 *centavos* (there are 100 *centavos* in a *real*). Although money and travellers' cheques can be exchanged in banks, *cambios* (exchange offices) and some hotels, the cheapest and most efficient method is to withdraw Brazilian currency direct from an ATM.

Check that you are able to withdraw cash with your debit card before leaving home. Most banks make a fixed charge for each withdrawal, so avoid making lots of small withdrawals. Although ATMs are found throughout the country, there are often just one or two machines in any particular bank branch that accept international cards (look for the symbol on the machine that matches the one on your card).

Credit cards are also widely accepted, although not as widely as in the US and Europe, for example. Small restaurants and hotels, particularly in some of the out-of-the-way destinations, will often only accept cash.

POSTAL AND INTERNET SERVICES

Postcards home will be slow (two weeks or more) but will generally arrive eventually. Post offices and post boxes are marked *Correios* and are blue and yellow. Your hotels will generally post your cards for you, but if you forget, there is a post office at the airport.

Many rental apartments have high-speed broadband, and internet access is widely available in hotels, where speeds range from just tolerable to more than acceptable. If you plan on bringing your own laptop, ask about free WiFi access in your hotel room before you book. Internet cafes are cheap and plentiful, but they are often crowded and overheated.

TIPS/GRATUITIES

✓ Yes ✗ No		
Restaurants (service included)	✗	
Cafes/bars waiting staff	✓	15%
Taxis	✓	round up fare
Concierges	✓	R$3–R$10
Tour guides	✓	R$3–R$10
Chambermaids	✓	R$20–R$30

TELEPHONES

Using your mobile phone from abroad is expensive for both national and international calls, but if you want to use it in Brazil, check before departure that both your handset will function, and that your operator and account is set up for roaming. If you intend to make a lot of local calls (or need to be contacted regularly in Brazil without international call access), it may be worth buying your own Brazilian mobile phone and SIM card.

To call Brazil from overseas, first use the international access code (00 for the UK), and then Brazil's international dialling code (55), followed by the area code, then the number.

Phone cards, available in news kiosks, are the cheapest way to make calls. Instructions are often given only in Portuguese.

Emergency telephone numbers
Police ☎ 190   Fire/Ambulance ☎ 193
Tourist Police ☎ (21) 2332-2924

International dialling codes
UK: 00 (21) 44   Netherlands: 00 (21) 31
Germany: 00 (21) 49   Mainland Spain: 00 (21) 34
USA and Canada: 00 (21) 1   Australia: 00 (21) 61

The number in brackets (21) is the "carrier code" for the phone company Embratel. Rates vary across carriers, but Embratel also offer operator-assisted dialling on 0800 703 2111.

EMBASSIES AND CONSULATES
UK: ☎ (21) 2555 9600   USA: ☎ (21) 2292 7117
Germany: ☎ (21) 2554 0004   Netherlands: ☎ (21) 2157 5400
France: ☎ (21) 3974 6699   Spain: ☎ (21) 2543 3200
                                 Australia: ☎ (21) 3824 4624

ELECTRICITY
Outlets are a mixture of 110 volts and 220 volts with two round-pin plugs and US-style two-pin flat plugs. Visitors from Europe and the US will need a world travel adaptor.

HEALTH ADVICE

Sun advice Drink plenty of water and take regular breaks when walking. Wear a high-factor sunscreen, even on a cloudy day.

Doctors and dentists Ask your hotel to recommend a reliable private doctor or dentist. Call your travel insurer as soon as you can.

Drugs Bring prescriptions for medicines you need. Pharmacies sell a wide range of drugs over the counter without controls. Be wary of their advice for all but minor ailments.

Water Tap water is generally safe to drink, although it is advisable to drink bottled water for at least the first few weeks after arriving.

PERSONAL SAFETY

Don't let paranoia ruin your visit. Rio has its high-crime "ghettos", and petty theft is common, but if you take sensible precautions, you are likely to have a safe, enjoyable holiday. Don't flash money or bulging wallets around, don't wear expensive jewellery if it's not appropriate to the situation, and be polite and confident when you are on the streets.

The tourist police in Rio (Avenida Afrânio de Melo Franco 159 in Leblon, opposite the Scala nightclub; tel: (21) 2332 2924) speak several languages and are particularly helpful when a crime needs to be reported for insurance purposes.

OPENING HOURS

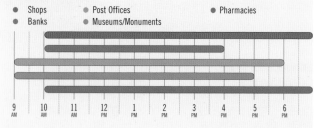

Many of Rio's large shopping centres are open as late as 10pm for shoppers (later for entertainment) and some are open on Sundays too. It is common for attractions like museums and cultural centres to close all day on Monday. There are 24-hour pharmacies in the city.

LANGUAGE

Portuguese is the national language. Nationals of Portugal will be understood, but Brazilian Portuguese is a language in its own right. Learning a few key phrases will help, and is not so difficult. Most Brazilians will understand you if you speak in Spanish, although you may have trouble understanding their reply.

Do you speak English?	*Você fala inglês?*	you're welcome	*de nada*
		today	*hoje*
I don't understand	*Eu não entendo*	yesterday	*ontem*
yes	*sim (pronounced as "seem")*	tomorrow	*amanhã*
		I'm sorry	*Desculpe*
no	*não (pronounced like "now", but with longer vowel)*	I'm lost	*Estou perdido*
		near/far	*perto/longe*
		left/right	*deixou/direito*
hello/goodbye	*oi/tchau*	straight on	*diretamente*
good morning	*bom dia*	open/closed	*abra/fechado*
good evening/night	*boa noite*	Where is...the bank	*Onde... o banco...é?*
please	*por favor*	How many kilometres?	*Quantos quilômetros?*
thank you	*obrigado/obrigada*		

pharmacy	*farmácia*	It hurts... here	*Machuca... aqui*
clinic	*clínica*	diarrhoea	*diarréia*
doctor	*médico*	dizziness	*vertigem*
medicine	*medicina*	Help!	*Socorro!*
pain	*dor*		

restaurant	*restaurante*	bread	*pão*
breakfast	*café da manhã*	butter	*manteiga*
lunch	*almoço*	coffee	*café*
dinner	*jantar*	fish	*peixe*
eggs	*ovos*	chicken	*galinha*

market	*mercado*	Do you have another colour?	*Tem outra cor?*
shop/store	*loja*		
How much is it?	*Quanto é ele?*	Where is the mirror?	*Onde o espelho é?*
It's expensive	*É caro*	enough	*bastante*

Best places to see

Cristo Redentor	36–37
Estádio do Maracanã	38–39
Jardim Botânico	40–41
Museu de Arte Moderna	42–43
Pão de Açúcar	44–45
Parque Nacional da Tijuca	46–47
Praça XV	48–49
Praia de Copacabana	50–51
Praia do Ipanema	52–53
Santa Teresa, Largo dos Guimarães	54–55

Cristo Redentor

www.corcovado.com.br

One of the Seven Wonders of the Modern World, the statue of Christ the Redeemer stands atop Corcovado, "Hunchback" mountain – 704m (2,310ft) of sheer rock that rises out of the Parque Nacional da Tijuca.

The art deco monument was designed by Frenchman Paul Landowski (1875–1961) and shipped block by block from France. Made of soapstone and cement, it is 30m (98ft) high.

The cog-driven train that makes the 20-minute ascent up Corcovado dates back to 1884. Within the Corcovado train station at the base, there is a small but interesting exhibition about the history of the train and statue. A taxi for two can cost the same as one train ticket (which includes admission to the statue. Taxi drivers at Corcovado will try to overcharge you, so consider taking one from your hotel. All taxis are required to wait at Paineiras Station halfway up, while visitors continue by van.

Where the train line ends (and where the vans drop you off) there are 220 steps to the very top of Corcovado; alternatively, you can take one of two escalators. When you get to the top drink in the panoramic view and join the throngs of tourists posing for the camera, with their arms outstretched in imitation of the statue. Signs point out some of the major landmarks. Just behind the statue, and easily missed, is a little chapel, Capela de Nossa Senhora da Aparedica, where Mass and wedding ceremonies take place.

✚ 16G ✉ Rua Cosme Velho 513, Cosme Velho ☎ (21) 2558 2359
🕐 Daily 8:30–6 ✋ Expensive 🍴 Café Trem ($) at the train station at the bottom sells drinks and snacks. There is also an inexpensive cafe at the top

2 Estádio do Maracanã

www.suderj.rj.gov.br/maracana

Constructed for the 1950 World Cup tournament, and still one of the largest stadiums in the world, the Maracanã is steeped in footballing legend.

The stadium is undergoing a US$400 million facelift in preparation for the 2014 World Cup. Both the stadium and the museum will be closed during the renovations and are due to reopen in 2013 for the Confederations Cup. The upgraded venue will feature new entrances and exits, and modern bars and restaurants. As a listed building, the facade will remain untouched, but an extended roof will cover the whole spectator area. Until then, football matches will be held in alternative stadiums in the city; check the website or visit the tourist office in Rio for the latest information.

Many games, including the World Cup final, are scheduled to be played in the upgraded venue, making the Maracanã

only the second stadium in the world, after Mexico's Estádio Azteca, to host the World Cup twice.

When the stadium does reopen it will be possible to visit for matches (normally on Sundays at 5pm) and on non-match days to take a tour of the stadium and The Museum of Football (which must be reserved in advance).

✚ 1C ✉ Rua Professor Eurico Rabelo Maracanã ☎ (21) 2568 9962

3 Jardim Botânico

www.jbrj.gov.br

In 1808, Dom João VI, king of Portugal, created these botanical gardens, which today form one of the most remarkable collections in the world. A visit here is a good option if it's raining, as the canopy of trees forms a natural umbrella.

The gardens are found in the exclusive district of the same name, with upmarket shops and restaurants. Pick up a leaflet with a map at one of the two entrances and take a leisurely stroll along the pathways. Walking through the lush greenery, you may spot tropical flowers such as orchids, and exotic birds, including parakeets and hummingbirds, as well as squirrels, marmosets and monkeys.

Don't miss the magnificent Avenue of Royal Palms and the enormous, 120-year old pau mulato tree.

You will see cocoa and banana trees and the enormous Vitoria regia water lily (all from the Amazon region) on Frei Leandro pond. Relax under a cherry tree by the carp-filled lake at the Japanese Corner and perhaps spend a quiet moment in the meditation area.

There are fountains and sculptures, including two fashioned in lead of the nymphs Echo and Narcissus, created by the great Brazilian artist, Mestre Valentim. Other key sights include the ruins of a gunpowder factory dating from 1808, an extensive library of botanical works and a greenhouse devoted to orchids.

➕ 14J ✉ Rua Jardim Botânico 1008 (also at 920) ☎ (21) 3874 1808 🕓 Daily 8–5 ✋ Inexpensive 🍴 Café Botânica ($; daily 8:30–5) ❓ Tours: daily 9–3:30, last 90 mins

4 Museu de Arte Moderna (MAM)

www.mamrio.com.br

The Museum of Modern Art in Rio is one of Latin America's most impressive modern art museums and an important example of postmodernist architecture.

The striking building sits on the waterfront of Guanabara Bay, next to Parque do Flamengo, its bold contemporary design in stark contrast to the soft organic lines of the green hills behind. It was designed by the great Brazilian architect Affonso Eduardo Reidy (1909–64), with angled concrete ribs supporting a light-filled interior space. From the upper floors, there are magnificent views of the gardens, designed by Brazilian landscape architect Roberto Burle Marx (1909–94).

Founded in 1948 by art enthusiasts, the Museu de Arte Moderna continues to play a vital role in the city's modern art scene and to nurture Brazilian artists. Disaster struck in 1978

when a fire devastated the museum, destroying most of the building as well as the majority of its exhibits. It was saved only when art patron Gilberto Chateaubriand donated his entire 4,000-piece collection in 1989.

The permanent exhibition now includes more than 11,000 paintings, sculptures and engravings by major Brazilian and international artists, such as Rodin, Brancusi and Picasso, with an inspiring programme of changing exhibitions.

MAM is very much a "living" museum, following the model of New York's Museum of Modern Art (MoMA). Masters in their field were called on to set up the museum's various disciplines; Candido Portinari (1903–62) was responsible for painting, Alcides Miranda (1909–2001) for architecture and Luís Heitor (1905–92) for music. Today, visitors can take part in art workshops, visit the museum's library and watch films from an archive that is one of the most important in Latin America.

➕ 10D ✉ Avenida Infante Dom Henrique 85, Parque do Flamengo
☎ (21) 2240 4944 🕐 Tue–Fri 12–6, Sat–Sun, holidays 12–7 (ticket office closes 30 mins before end of visiting hours) ✋ Inexpensive 🍴 Laguiole restaurant (Mon–Fri 12–5) ❓ Book and gift shop, Barma (Mon–Fri 12–6, Sat–Sun 12–7)

5 Pão de Açúcar (Sugarloaf Mountain)

www.bondinho.com.br

The world-famous Sugarloaf Mountain rises 395m (1,296ft) from a small peninsula looking out onto Guanabara Bay. The enjoyable ascent by cable car affords beautiful views over the cityscape, the beaches and the hills.

The cable car, inaugurated in 1912, was the very first in Brazil, and one of only three in the world at that time. Augusto Ferreira Ramos was the Brazilian engineer responsible for the idea, which used local labour and German technology. It was extensively rebuilt in 1973. A small exhibition at the entrance includes historical photographs and scale models.

Sugarloaf is just one of many *morros* (hills) that line the coast of Guanabara Bay. It rises between the two smaller hills of Morro da Urca and Cara de Cão. The two-stage cable-car journey departs every 20 minutes and takes just three minutes per stage. The cars each hold 65 passengers and are fully glazed to allow sweeping panoramic vistas; they do have a tendency to sway in the wind. Try to visit on a cloud-free day and just before sunset for the best views. Avoid mid-morning and mid afternoon when most of the tour groups seem to arrive.

The first cable car travels up Morro da Urca (218m/715ft), where there is a cafe/restaurant with a terrace, a small playground, some overpriced souvenir shops and a helipad. The second leg, up to Morro de Pão de Açúcar, gives the most spectacular views.

✚ 24G ✉ Avenida Pasteur 520
☎ (21) 2461 2700 🕐 Daily 8–7:50
✋ Expensive 🍴 Cafe/restaurant with terrace after the first cable car

6 Parque Nacional da Tijuca

Tijuca National Park, which stretches up from Jardim Botânico (▶ 40–41), contains the largest urban forest in the world, and is a cool, green retreat from the heat of the city below.

Much of the park is made up of the ancient and rare Mata Atlântica (Atlantic rainforest), which once covered the coast for hundreds of kilometres in all directions. Public transport to Tijuca is difficult, and although there is a good network of paths it is easy to get lost, even with a map, so it's a good idea to take a half-day jeep and walking tour with guide, arranged through your hotel or local tour agency (try to avoid weekends, which can be busy with locals). Some of the highlights include the viewpoints of Mirante Dona Marta, Vista Chinesa and Mesa do Imperador; the 30m-high (98ft) waterfall, Cascatinha do Taunay; and the slightly smaller Cascata Diamantina. Fascinating pockets of history can be found at the pink wooden chapel, Capela Mayrink, dating from 1863, and the **Museu do Açude.** This 19th-century building was renovated in 1920 in neo-colonial style. Here you'll find an impressive collection of Portuguese tiles, period furniture and Oriental art.

The highest point in the park is Pico da Tijuca (1,021m/ 3,350ft), which can be reached on a short walk. Bom Retiro (658m/2,159ft) is a good picnic spot; alternatively, you can have lunch at Os Esquilos restaurant ($$$; Estrada Barão d'Escragnolle s/n; tel: (21) 2492 2197; Tue–Sun 12–6; follow signs from the park's main gate).

✚ 13H
Museu do Açude
✉ Estrada do Açude 764, Alto da Boa Vista ☎ (21) 2492 5443; www.museuscastromaya.com.br
🕐 Wed–Mon 11–5. Closed all major holidays ✋ Inexpensive

7 Praça XV

Praça Quinze de Novembro, or Praça XV as it is more commonly written, lies at the heart of Rio's old town, Centro Histórico.

Named for 15 November 1889, when Brazil turned its back on the royal family and declared itself a Republic, the square was originally the city's main venue for large public events, from parades to bullfights – a tradition that has been revived in recent years, with the square hosting a number of cultural events.

The **Paço Imperial,** with its small cultural centre, library and permanent and temporary art exhibitions, dominates the square. This building started out in 1743 as home to the Governor of Rio, but began a new life as a royal palace after the arrival of the royal family in 1808. It was here that Princess Isabel signed the momentous Lei Áurea (Golden Law), which abolished slavery in Brazil.

Just off the square is the imposing **Palácio Tiradentes,** home to the Brazilian Congress when Rio was the capital (1926–60). Now the seat of the legislative

assembly, it contains a few photographic and multimedia exhibits, but the building's exterior, particularly the splendid dome, is the main attraction.

Adjacent to Praça XV is the Arco do Teles (arch), which leads to the pedestrianized street of Travessa do Comércio. This is dotted with tiny bars and *sobrados*, colonial two- and three-storey buildings with traditional ironwork balconies. Pick any one of the charming open-air bars where locals throng after work (weekdays only).

✚ 10B ⬛ Cais do Oriente ($$; ➤ 90)

Paço Imperial

✉ Praça XV ☎ (21) 2533 4407 🕐 Tue–Sun 12–6 ✋ Inexpensive

Palácio Tiradentes

✉ Rua Primeiro de Março ☎ (21) 2588 1411 🕐 Mon–Sat 10–5, Sun 12–5 ✋ Free ℹ Guided tours Mon–Fri

Praia de Copacabana

Playground of the rich and famous in the 1950s, Copacabana beach still resounds with echoes of those glamorous days, attracting huge numbers of Brazilians and foreign visitors to its international hotels and thriving beach culture.

As if painted with the flourish of a master's brush, Copacabana sweeps around gracefully in a 4km-long (2.5-mile) crescent of white sand giving way to turquoise water. High-rise international hotels and expensive accommodation blocks are set back from the beach, which throngs with people all through the day. Bronzed pensioners power walk or play cards, while *capoeira* performers show off their acrobatic martial-arts dance. Skilled football and *futevolei* (foot volley) players compete on the sands, while in the surf, the offspring of Rio's middle classes splash around with the children of the *favelas* (shanty towns). For the daily influx of newly arrived tourists, it is an exciting place.

The lifeguard posts *(postos)* that stand sentinel along the length of the beach double as landmarks, beginning at Posto 1 close to the Morro do Leme end. Postos 2 and 3 in front of the Copacabana Palace tend to attract foreign tourists; at Posto 4 is a children's football school, while Posto 5 is usually a quiet spot. At Posto 6, near the fort, are the boats and nets used by the fishermen who head out early in the morning to get their daily catch. Here, a lifelike bronze statue of Carlos Drummond de Andrade – a revered Brazilian poet – sits on a pavement bench. Copa's beach kiosks (much smarter than those in Ipanema) offer snacks and delicious chilled coconut water, and have well-kept toilets and baby-changing facilities built underground.

Although Copacabana beach is now well lit at night, you are advised not to walk along the beach after dark. Beach vendors can be particularly persistent at Copacabana and may try to overcharge.

✚ 19M–21J

9 Praia do Ipanema

Ipanema's palm-fringed beach is bookended by the "Two Brothers" mountain to the west and Arpoador rock to the east. As urban beaches go, this is perhaps the world's most beautiful.

Postos (lifeguard posts) along the beach, as in Copacabana, serve as landmarks and meeting points, and many attract a distinct clientele. Posto 9 is where a younger, hipper crowd tends to gather, while Posto 8, marked by a huge rainbow flag, is a gay hangout. The part of the beach closest to Arpoador tends to attract families; on the jutting rock itself, a crowd gathers every evening to celebrate the glorious sunset.

Running parallel to the beach is Rua Visconde de Pirajá, Ipanema's main shopping street, lined with fashion boutiques, bookshops and juice bars. The area's leafy squares and side streets – dotted with chic boutiques and art galleries – invite wandering and people-watching.

Do what the locals do and set up camp near the beach bar of your choice. Beach vendors will rent you chairs and umbrellas and bring you drinks and food all day long; note that overcharging can be a problem. Other

beach vendors patrol the sands selling everything from ice
cream and the legendary crunchy "Globo" biscuits (➤ 60),
to corn on the cob and cheese on a stick.

On Sunday, the beachfront road is closed to traffic, and fills
with walkers, cyclists and lithe young things on rollerblades.
At weekends and on holidays the beach becomes particularly
crowded. Currents can be dangerous at times – Ipanema means
"bad water" in the indigenous Tupi Guarani language – so even
experienced swimmers should take heed of lifeguard warnings
and follow sensible precautions.

✚ 16M–18M

10 Santa Teresa, Largo dos Guimarães

The triangular-shaped plaza of Largo dos Guimarães, surrounded by bars and restaurants, lies at the heart of lovely, laid-back Santa Teresa – a bohemian hangout reached by a rickety old tram from Centro.

Sitting in the cool green hills, the neighbourhood of Santa Teresa, with its historic buildings, craft shops and charming restaurants, typically Brazilian but also offering international food, is sometimes described as the Montmartre of Rio. Largo dos Guimarães is its unofficial centre. Every so often, local musicians spill out of the tram and hold impromptu musical events in the square.

Most people visit Santa Teresa on a day trip, making Largo dos Guimarães their first stop, although an increasing number are making their base here in boutique hotels and hostels that benefit from the cool hilltop air on humid days.

Call in at the delightful courtyard cafe Jasmin Manga for a *cafezinho* (little coffee) under the bamboo, before visiting the tiny **Cine Santa Teresa** across the road. The single-screen theatre, with just 46 seats, is the venue for independent and Brazilian films, as well as changing events and social projects. An unofficial tourist information centre operates in the foyer, and a small art gallery, Cine Gallery, hosts changing exhibitions.

The steep steps up from Largo dos Guimarães lead to a local ballet school and community centre with a small bookshop. It's a venue for special occasions and cultural events; if you hear music it is worth a wander up the steps to take a look. If you don't want to take the tram back, you can easily pick up a taxi in the square.

✚ 7D
Cine Santa Teresa
✉ Rua Paschoal Carlos Magno, 136, Largo do Guimarães
☎ (21) 2222 0203; www.cinesanta.com.br

Best things to do

Top activities   58–59

Best snacks   60–61

Beautiful beaches   62–62

Top ten drinks   64–65

Best buys   66–67

Stunning views   68–69

Places to take the children 70–71

Green retreats   72–73

Best for live music   74–75

Top activities

Climbing
Hire a guide and scale the heights of Pão de Açúcar (Sugarloaf Mountain; ➤ 44–45) and Corcovado (➤ 36–37), or the challenging Pedra da Gávea, accessed from Barra da Tijuca (➤ 172).

Cycling
Rent a bike and pedal around the 7.5km (4.5-mile) track encircling Lagoa Rodrigo de Freitas (➤ 125), enjoy car-free Sundays on the beachfront roads, or head further afield.

Football
Brazil's national sport is played out on the beaches and in parks all over the city. Even with limited Portuguese, it's relatively easy to join in, or just get yourself a football and start a game yourself.

Hang-gliding
Fly like a bird in a tandem hang-gliding flight, jumping off at Tijuca forest and floating down onto the beach below.

Hiking
Trek through the rainforest of Parque Nacional da Tijuca (➤ 46–47) with a guide or follow the scenic, shady trail of Pista Cláudio Coutinho in Urca (➤ 116–117).

Outdoor gyms
Locals treat the whole of Rio as an outdoor gym, but there are also exercise stations on the beaches for stretching, pull-ups and chin-ups, with fully equipped weight gyms popping up too.

Sailing
Take out a pedalo or rowing boat on Lagoa Rodrigo de Freitas (➤ 125) or charter a private yacht from the Marina da Glória (➤ 105).

Surfing
Although the inner-city beaches of Ipanema and Copacabana do have some surf, the sheer number of swimmers means safety is an issue. Most surfers head out to the western beaches, particularly Prainha (➤ 174).

Walking
Join the power walkers who pound the pavements at any time of day, but particularly early morning and late afternoon when the sun is cooler.

Yoga
In this body-obsessed city, fitness classes abound. Yoga is a popular choice, with classes in centres throughout the city, but also on the beach and even in the Botanic Gardens (➤ 40–41).

Best snacks

Acarajé

Although this African-influenced snack is typical of the state of Bahia, it is widely found in Rio. It's a patty of fried beans with shrimp and spicy sauce and is one of the city's staple street foods.

Biscoitos Globo

Even if you don't find the ubiquitous Globo biscuits particularly tasty, you'll be constantly reminded of them as beach vendors hawk these air-puffed rings in green (salty) or red (sweet) packets.

Bolinhos de bacalhau

These bite-sized cod fish balls are just one of many *petiscos* (snacks) Brazilians eat as a pre-dinner accompaniment to a glass of cold beer.

Bolo de rolo

Most Brazilians have a sweet tooth and love their *bolos* (cakes), which come in many different flavours. *Bolo de rolo* (cake roll), made with *doce de goiaba* (guava marmalade), is a particular favourite.

Caldo

Caldo comes in two varieties: *verde* (green), with potatoes, onions and kale, and *feijao* (black bean), sometimes with added sausage. Although it can be ordered in a bowl in restaurants, *caldo* is often served in shot glasses in bars with drinks, and even on the beach as a quick snack.

Carne de sol

"Sun beef" is beef that has been salted and dried in the sun. Originating from the northeast, it is served throughout Rio as a delicious bar snack.

Empanadas
The classic Brazilian snack, these small crescent-shaped pies are typically filled with *frango* (chicken), *palmito* (heart of palm) or *camarão* (prawn).

Pão de queijo
Mini, melt-in-the-mouth cheese breads are found in juice bars and *lanchonettes* (snack bars) all over Rio.

Pastel
These delicious little pastries, filled with *frango* (chicken), *carne* (ground beef) and *catipury* (cream cheese), are sold on the streets and beaches of Rio.

Torta de limão
Both sweet and tart, lime pie made with sweetened condensed milk and limes is one of Brazil's most popular desserts.

Beautiful beaches

Barra de Guaratiba
A favourite film location, this 2km-long (1.2-mile) beach is backed by marshlands and trails to a trio of deserted beaches: Inferno, Perigoso and Meio (➤ 173).

Barra da Tijuca
The white sands of seemingly endless "Barra" stretch for 16km (10 miles) along the turquoise waters of the Atlantic coast (➤ 172).

Grumari
Backed by steep green mountains, dense vegetation and rare *catinga* (coastal scrub), beautfiul Grumari is part of an environmental protection zone. A small part of it, Abricó, is a nudist beach (➤ 172–173).

Praia de Copacabana
This huge crescent of sand, one of the most famous urban beaches in the world, throngs with people day and night. It's a great spot for sunbathing, relaxing and generally admiring the scene (➤ 50–51).

Praia do Ipanema
Much-photographed Ipanema is physically blessed – it is fringed by palm trees, with twin green hills at the western end and three pretty islands in the bay. Sunset from the eastern rock of Arpoador is a sight to remember (➤ 52–53).

Praia do Leblon
A channel of water, Jardim de Alá, divides Ipanema's beach from Leblon's. It is one of the quietest of all the city beaches, surrounded by exclusive apartment blocks and with a children's play area on the sands (➤ 142).

Praia do Pepê
This little corner of Barra da Tijuca beach (between Postos 1 and 2), is a trendy local hangout, and is particularly popular with surfers and kite-surfers (➤ 172).

Praia Vermelha
Backed by coconut and bamboo trees and the green hill of Morro da
Urca, the pinkish hues of the sands here give "Red Beach" its name
(➤ 116–117).

Prainha
The small but perfectly formed "Little Beach" is a secluded spot.
Pounded by the Atlantic surf, it is often deserted during the week,
apart from the occasional dedicated surfer (➤ 174).

Recreio dos Bandeirantes
"Pioneer's Playground" is a wild expanse of sand backed by lush green
vegetation and is a real haven for those in search of solitude (➤ 175).

Top ten drinks

Açai

This dark purple fruit of an Amazonian palm tree is one of the most nutritional foods on earth and Rio's most fashionable drink. Join surfers and health freaks who drink the frozen juice and pulp with ice, or eat it out of a bowl with granola.

Agua de Coco

Delicious and hydrating, a *bem gelado* (really cold) coconut water is the perfect way to cool down on a hot Rio day, or to revive yourself after one too many *caipirinhas*.

Batida

Fruit juice, *cachaça* (or sometimes vodka) and condensed milk are mixed up with crushed ice to create this uniquely Brazilian cocktail. Try an unusual, though popular *batida de caju*, which is made with cashew juice.

Brazilian wine

Traditionally, Brazil hasn't been known for its wine, but some restaurants and bars are now serving some fine reds, such as Miolo, and some excellent sparkling wines, including Aurora.

Cafezinho

An important social ritual as much as a drink, locals like a *cafezinho* (little coffee) morning, noon and night.

Caipirinha

No one should miss the chance to sample the Brazilian

national cocktail. For a variation on the classic *cachaça*, lime and ice concoction, try one *con maracujá* (with fresh passionfruit).

Chopp
Cariocas (locals) take their *chopp* (draught beer) very seriously indeed and it is by far the most popular alcoholic drink in the city.

Guárana
This energy-giving drink made from an Amazonian berry is sold in distinctive green cans throughout Brazil.

Matte Leão
The Brazilian version of iced tea is sold throughout the city, but particularly on the beaches. Try it with lime *(com limao)*.

Suco
In Rio, you are never far away from a *casa de sucos* (juice bar). Their menus of tropical juices are almost endless: try a classic combination of *abacaxi com hortelã* (pineapple with mint) or a juice made from exotic fruits such as taperabá, sapoti or acerola.

Best buys

Beachwear
Audacious and infamous, the bikini is the closest Brazil gets to a uniform. Shops like BumBum (► 150) and Salinas (Rua Visconde de Pirajá 547) stock the most imaginative designs.

Brazilian hammock
Bring home a colourful, fringed Brazilian hammock, picking one that's hand-woven, 100 per cent cotton and, ideally, fair trade.

Cachaça
A bottle of the potent Brazilian spirit brewed from pure sugar cane can cost anything from a few *reals* to several thousand. Vist the Academia da Cachaça (► 151) to sample and purchase some of the finest brands around, or stock up on cheap and cheerful Pitú and Number 51 from any supermarket.

Cristo Redentor statue
Buy a miniature Christ the Redeemer figure in wood or soapstone as a kitsch reminder of your trip. They are sold all over the city, but avoid

purchasing them at the attraction itself, where they are around double the price.

Football shirts
Everyone loves the Brazilian football team. Green and yellow vests and football shirts can be bought cheaply from market stalls throughout the city; those made of better quality fabric can be purchased from sports shops and at the airport.

Gemstones
Buy Brazilian gems such as the dazzling purple topaz, unworked or fashioned into jewellery from reputable shops such as H. Stern (► 141) and Amsterdam Sauer (► 141).

Handicrafts Artesanato Brasileiro (Brazilian crafts)
Pieces handcrafted by local artisans are a better alternative to mass-produced gifts. Try to buy fair trade from specialist shops such as Pé de Boi (Rua Ipiranga 55) and Loja Artíndia (► 112).

Havaianas
Practical and pretty, compact and light, Brazilian flip-flops are the perfect souvenir. Go for a classic design with a tiny Brazilian flag, or chose from the new styles that are launched every year.

Music
Take home the soundtrack of your Rio holiday. Shops such as Toca do Vinicius (► 150) allow you to listen before you buy.

Vintage and antique items
Look for crystal chandeliers, vintage clothes and hardwood furniture in the shops on Rua do Lavradio, which hosts an antique street market, Feira Rio Antigo, every Saturday (► 91).

Stunning views

Arpoador (► 136)

Cristo Redentor (► 36–37)

Forte de Copacabana (► 115)

Mirante do Leblon (► 140)

Museu da Chácara do Céu (► 98)

Pão de Açúcar (➤ 44–45)

Parque da Catacumba (➤ 127)

Parque da Cidade (➤ 128)

Parque Nacional da Tijuca (➤ 46–47)

Rocinha (➤ 145)

Places to take the children

Baixo Bebê
At Posto 12 on Leblon beach (➤ 142), "Low Baby" is an area dedicated to babies and young children, with play areas, plenty of toys, changing facilities and welcome shade.

Boat trip
Take to the waters of Guanabara Bay, and hear stories of the pirates, native Indians and explorers who once patrolled the shores.

Bonde
Swaying up to Pão de Açúcar (➤ 44–45) in a cable car looking down on the city and beaches below is a fun trip for both adults and children.

Bondinho
Ride the little yellow tram (➤ 94) across the whitewashed aqueduct of Los Arcos up the hill to Santa Teresa, where you can buy a miniature replica as a souvenir in one of the many local craft shops.

Forte de Copacabana
Let little ones run around this hulking fort (➤ 115) built on the eve of World War I, climbing over the German Krupp cannons and exploring the domed bunker below with its reconstructed officers' quarters and army hospital ward.

Museu do Índio
Rio's most child-friendly museum (➤ 106), located in a two-storey mansion with garden, contains fascinating objects and photographs relating to Brazil's indigenous

population. There is also a shop selling arts and crafts, from ceramics and feathers to books and CDs, many of which will appeal to children.

Parque Nacional da Tijuca
Take your kids into the dense forest of Tijuca National Park (➤ 46–47) spotting plants and animals and perhaps taking a dip in one of the cooling pools.

Planetário
Rio's planetarium (➤ 129) is both enjoyable and educational. Its exhibits, including interactive games, appeal to children of most ages.

Rocinha
Show your offspring how the other half lives with a guided tour around the *favela* (shanty town) of Rocinha (➤ 145), where local children fly their home-made kites from the summit.

Train
Chug uphill through the jungle to Cristo Redentor (➤ 36–37) on Rio's historic cog-driven railway. Walk, or take an elevator or escalator, to the summit, where the must-see, iconic Christ statue quite literally will welcome you and your children with open arms.

Green retreats

Instituto Moreira Salles
Wander around the cool interior spaces filled with impressive exhibits at the exquisite Moreira Salles Institute (➤ 126); relax in the museum's outdoor cafe next to a blue pool surrounded by delightful gardens created by the great Brazilian landscape designer Roberto Burle Marx.

Jardim Botânico
Despite their central location, the Botanic Gardens (➤ 40–41) are a world away from the rest of the city, with exuberant vegetation, colourful blooms and imperial palms contributing to an oasis of calm. Founded in 1808, the extensive gardens showcase the enormous variety of Brazilian flora.

Parque da Catacumba
A walk up the steeply sloping Catacombs Park (➤ 127), dotted with sculptures by Brazilian artists, takes you through tropical forest overlooking the coast and mountains below.

Parque do Flamengo
This waterside city park, in the neighbourhood of Flamengo, was designed by Roberto Burle Marx, and is a real green lung, attracting cyclists and joggers and dotted with amenities from roller-skating rinks to children's playgrounds.

Parque Nacional da Tijuca
The sprawling national park (➤ 46–47), which includes the world's largest urban forest, is just one of the

cariocas' (locals') playgrounds. They come to relax, hike, cool off in the clear rivers and waterfalls and even rock climb and hang-glide.

Pista Cláudio Coutinho

This hidden trail (► 116–117) flanked by tropical trees and steep green mountains is a world away from the city hustle and bustle where you can stroll next to the sea, spotting colourful birds and cheeky monkeys.

Quinta da Boa Vista

The "Park of the Good View" (► 86) is rich in history. Once part of a Jesuit farm, it went on to become a garden for Brazilian emperors and today is a well used public park, particularly popular with families at weekends.

Sítio de Burle Marx

A superlative creation from Brazil's master landscaper, the Burle Marx Gardens (► 173) have a painterly quality, lovingly decorated with tropic al plants and flowers. The grounds are filled with several thousand species, many of them endangered, as well as pools and waterfalls.

Best for live music

The beach and the street

Rio is alive with music and you are never far away from an impromptu performance. The lilting melodies of wandering musicians can be heard in the street and on the beach, with the beautiful city as a backdrop.

Bip Bip

This tiny neighbourhood bar (➤ 124) has been hosting live samba and bossa nova in the city for as long as anyone can remember.

Carnaval rehearsals

Even if you are not in Rio for the event itself, you can still experience the deafening beat of the *bateria* (drum section) and some of the mounting excitement. Rehearsals take place throughout the city between August and February. Check with the tourist office, Riotur, for the latest information.

Gafieiras

Atmospheric samba clubs known as *gafieiras,* such as Rio Scenarium (Rua do Lavradio 20; www.rioscenarium.com.br) and Centro Cultural Carioca (➤ 92) throb with live music and dance most nights.

Oi Noites Cariocas

"Rio Nights" is a programme of pop and rock concerts that take place at Pier Mauá (Avenida Rodrigues Alves 10, Centro; www.piermauasa. com.br) during January and February.

Plataforma 1

Admittedly touristy, this Carnaval-style samba show with plenty of singing and dancing is high energy and good fun. It can be booked through most tour agencies and hotels; just avoid the mediocre dinner.
✉ Rua Adalberto Ferreira 32, Leblon ☎ (21) 2274 4022 ⊙ Daily 10pm

Sala Cecilia Meireles

One of the city's most important venues for chamber music, this concert hall is an intimate space offering a high standard of performances.
✉ Largo da Lapa 47 ☎ (21) 2332 9176; www.salaceciliameireles.com.br

Sambódromo

Look out for occasional music concerts by some of the world's best international performers, which have included Madonna, Elton John and The Rolling Stones (➤ 10).

Theatro Municipal

A full programme of classical music, opera and ballet takes place at Rio's historic municipal theatre (➤ 88). Concerts and performances are enormously popular, so try to book ahead as far as possible (direct through the box office or via the website).

Toca do Vinicius

The lovely owner of this music shop puts on free samba and choro performances on the pavement outside. Check in the shop or on the website for the latest schedule (➤ 150).

Exploring

Centro and São Cristóvão   79–92

Santa Teresa and Lapa   93–102

Guanabara Bay to   103–112
Tijuca Forest

Copacabana and Urca   113–124

Lagoa   125–134

Ipanema   135–151

Rio's beaches get all the attention, and much of it is deserved, but the city's extraordinary natural beauty, which includes huge swathes of mountain greenery and pockets of quiet, attractive parkland, is not confined to its sandy shore.

Rio's – and indeed the country's – main cultural corridor lies in the old Centro Histórico (Historic Centre). Here is a dense concentration of colonial churches, museums, galleries and cultural centres, although quite a few of the historic buildings are in need of repair and are dwarfed by some rather modern monstrosities. Of monster proportions, but loved by all Brazilians, is the football mecca of the Maracanã – one of the world's most famous stadiums. High in the city's hills, the charming neighbourhood of Santa Teresa invites browsing in its craft shops and long, lazy lunches in its bohemian restaurants.

For visitors, the boundless energy and open outlook of the Cariocas (Rio locals), adds to all these highlights. It's little wonder they call this place the *cidade maravilhosa* (marvellous city).

Centro and São Cristóvão

Wander the streets of Rio's Centro Histórico, visiting colonial churches, convents and cathedrals, vibrant cultural centres and pretty *praças* (squares). The historic centre may be crumbling in parts and somewhat eclipsed by the seductive beaches, but this is its birthplace and still very much at the heart of the city.

Spend at least several hours, if not the whole day, breathing in some of Rio's history, taking time to relax at a pavement cafe and enjoying some of the city's cultural highlights. At the end of the day, join the office workers who gather for a cold beer in the historic centre's bars, many over a century old. If time is tight, consider an organized tour with a guide (most speak several languages), or, if you want to go it alone, visit the sights on foot, following the walk route (➤ 84–85), arriving either by metro, taxi or bus.

CATEDRAL METROPOLITANA

Dedicated to St Sebastian, the city's patron saint, the Metropolitan Cathedral's distinctive design was a creation of architect Edgar de Oliveira de Fonseca, who, according to one theory, was inspired by the Mayan pyramids. It takes the shape of a 100m-high (328ft) truncated cone, and is sometimes rather unkindly described as an upside-down coffee cup. Enter through the 18m-high (59ft) door and you will find yourself in a cavernous interior with space for 20,000 people, bathed in the mottled coloured light that comes through the full-height, stained-glass windows. A museum of sacred art (Tue–Thu 2–6; free) in the basement contains Dom Pedro II's throne and the fonts used to baptize the royal princes.

www.catedral.com.br

🏛 9C ✉ Avenida República de Chile 245, Centro
☎ (21) 2240 2669 🕐 Daily 7–6 ✋ Free ❓ Mass Sat–Sun at 10, Mon, Wed, Fri at 11, Tue, Thu at 9

ESTÁDIO DO MARACANÃ

Best places to see, ➤ 38–39.

IGREJA E MOSTEIRO DE SÃO BENTO

The church and monastery of St. Bento, founded in 1590 by Benedictine monks, lies to the north of Praça XV. Step inside to see its splendid baroque interior, with impressive gold and carved wood details, or listen to the Gregorian chanting at Sunday morning Mass at 10am and evening hymns (Sat 5pm, Sun 5:30pm).

www.osb.org.br

✚ 9A ✉ Rua Dom Gerardo 68, Centro ☎ (21) 2206 8100 🕐 Daily 7–6 ✋ Free

IGREJA NOSSA SENHORA DO MONTE DO CARMO

The Church of Our Lady of Monte do Carmo served as the city's cathedral from 1808 until 1976, when the much larger Catedral Metropolitana was inaugurated. Often simply called "Antiga Sé" (Old Cathedral), it has played a pivotal role in Rio's history, serving as the royal chapel during the 19th century. It was here that Prince Regent João VI was consecrated as King of Portugal in 1816 and where Dom Pedro I and Princess Leopoldina of Habsburg had their wedding blessing. It is believed that some of the remains of Pedro Álvares Cabral, the first European to reach Brazil's shores, are buried in the church's crypt.

✚ 9B ✉ Rua Primeiro de Março s/n, Centro ☎ (21) 2242 7766 🕐 Mon–Fri 8–6 ✋ Free

IGREJA DA ORDEM TERCEIRA DO CARMO

Separated from the old cathedral by only a tiny passageway is the
Church of the Third Order. The building dates back to 1770; the twin
towers of the church, decorated with traditional Portuguese *azulejos*
(tiles) were added later. Of note is the delicate carving in the interior,
particularly in the chapel and on the high altar. It was completed by Luis
Rosa da Fonseca, and Valentim da Fonseca e Silva (who later became
known as Mestre (Master) Valentim), at the end of the 18th century.

✚ 9B ✉ Rua Primeiro de Março s/n, Centro ☎ (21) 2242 4828 ⏰ Mon–Fri 8–3:30
✋ Free

ILHA FISCAL

Take a guided one-hour boat tour from Espaço Cultural Da Marinha
(Avenida Alfredo Agache; tel: (21) 2104 6025) to Ilha Fiscal, a vivid
green, neo-gothic castle in the bay of Baía de Guanabara. It was built in
1889 as a customs house and taken over by the navy in 1913. Today it
contains exhibitions relating to its history.

✚ 11A ✉ Avenida Alfredo Agache, Centro ☎ (21) 2104 6721 ⏰ Thu–Sun 1,
2:30 and 4 ✋ Moderate

MUSEU HISTÓRICO NACIONAL

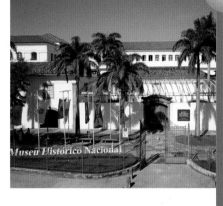

Rio's natural history museum, created in 1922, is one of the city's most impressive in terms of its exhibits and how they are presented. Set in tropical gardens, the museum is made up of several buildings, each with its own architectural style. These grew up in place of the 16th-century sea fort built by Rio's first Governor. The museum pieces, which number nearly 300,000, are an eclectic mix, ranging from indigenous headdresses and jewellery to items of religious art and numerous armaments.

www.museuhistoriconacional.com.br

🕂 10C ✉ Praça Marechal Âncora, Centro ☎ (21) 2550 9220 🕐 Tue–Fri 10–5:30, Sat–Sun, holidays 2–6 💧 Moderate

a walk around the Centro Histórico

This short walk covers a compact area, yet takes in a variety of key sights, from churches to cultural centres. It begins on a hilltop at Rio's magnificent monastery of São Bento and ends at the Arco do Teles, just off the historic square of Praça XV.

Begin at the Igreja e Mosteiro de São Bento (➤ 81). It is a good idea to get a taxi here (as the monastery stands on its own, you will avoid retracing your steps), although you still will have to walk, or take the elevator up the hill on which it stands. The monastery's peaceful location belies its dazzling interior.

Walk down the hill, and straight along Rua Primeiro de Março for 350m (380yds), with the water of Guanabara Bay to your left, to arrive at Praça Pio X.

The square is dominated by Igreja Nossa Senhora da Candelária (Mon–Fri 8–4, Sat–Sun 8–noon), one of the tallest churches in Rio. It was built between 1775 and 1898; note the magnificent cupola.

Get back onto Rua Primeiro de Março 66, just beyond Praça Pio X. On the left is the

Centro Cultural Banco do Brasil (▶ 92).

As well as hosting changing art exhibitions, this cultural centre, cafe and shop is a popular meeting place.

Continue down Rua Primeiro de Março to Praça XV.

This sprawling square is a major historic sight and home to a number of significant buildings. Pause by the granite and marble fountain, Chafariz do Mestre Valentim, built in 1789, which is also known as Chafariz da Pirâmide (Fountain of the Pyramid), because of its shape.

Walk towards the the edge of the square, with Guanabara Bay on your right, to the small Arco do Teles (arch), which leads to the narrow passageway of Travessa do Comércio.

Admire the wrought-iron balconies and traditional colonial *sobrados* (multistorey buildings) on this street, looking out for No. 13, which was once the home of Carmen Miranda, samba singer and Hollywood film star.

Distance 1.3km (0.8 miles)
Time 3 hours (including visits to sights, but not lunch)
Start point Igreja e Mosteiro de São Bento ✚ 9A
End point Praça XV ✚ 10B
Lunch Cais do Oriente ($$; ▶ 90)

MUSEU NACIONAL

Brazil's National Museum is one of Latin America's most significant natural history museums. Set up by Dom João VI in 1818 as a scientific institution, today it forms part of the Federal University of Rio de Janeiro. It is housed in the grand, neoclassical Palacio de São Cristóvāo, at one time known as the "Versailles of the Tropics". It is set in Quinta da Boa Vista (Park of the Good View). Once the main residence of the Portuguese Royal family, it is surrounded by extensive gardens landscaped in the French romantic style, with lawns, trees and a lake. Of late it has become rather down-at-heel, but now the palace and gardens are being restored.

Visitors to the museum can see exhibits divided into six main subject areas – Anthropology, Botany, Geology/Palaeontology, Entomology, Invertebrates and Vertebrates. The several thousand artefacts can seem overwhelming and the categories rather academic, so concentrate on the more obviously interesting displays, such as the exotic stuffed animals, or ceramics and other items relating to Brazil's two chief pre-Columbian cultures, Tupinambá and Guarani. It is also possible to see a few of the rooms in the palace, complete with their

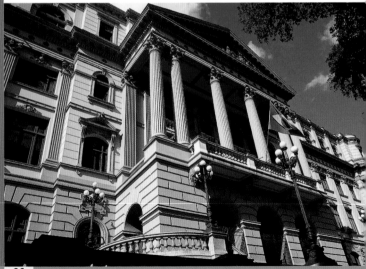

original interiors. A trip to the museum could be combined with a look at Rio's Zoo, the Jardim Zoológico (www.rio.rj.gov.br/web/riozoo), which lies just behind the palace at Quinta da Boa Vista.

www.museunacional.ufrj.br

✚ 2B ✉ Quinta da Boa Vista, São Cristóvão ☎ (21) 2562 6900 ⏰ Tue–Sun 10–4 ✋ Inexpensive

MUSEU NACIONAL DE BELAS ARTES

Rio's National Museum of Fine Arts, inspired by the Louvre in Paris, was built between 1908 and 1923. Many of the exhibits were originally brought over as part of the French Artistic Mission in 1816, an initiative by Dom João VI to create an archive of European masterpieces. The collection comprises nearly 20,000 pieces, including engravings, paintings, sculpture, and drawings, as well as decorative art, furniture and medals. Highlights from its permanent collection are prints by Chagall and Picasso and paintings by Brazilian artists such as Candido Portinari and Vitor Meireles. Temporary exhibitions are held throughout the year.

www.mnba.gov.br

✚ 9C ✉ Avenida Rio Branco 199, Centro ☎ (21) 2240 0068 ⏰ Tue–Fri 10–6, Sat–Sun, holidays 10–5 ✋ Inexpensive

PRAÇA XV

Best places to see, ➤ 48–49.

THEATRO MUNICIPAL

The Municipal Theatre is one of the most exquisite opera houses in Brazil. The sumptuous 1909 Beaux Arts building is modelled on the Paris Opera House and is highly decorated inside and out with fine stained glass, elegant chandeliers and gilt mirrors. The theatre reopened its doors to the public in 2010 after two years of extensive renovation work. Guided tours can be arranged (tel: (21) 2332 9220), but try to visit for a performance to see the building at its best.

www.theatromunicipal.rj.gov.br

➕ 9C ➕ Praça Marechal Floriano, Centro ☎ (21) 2332 9191 🕐 Varies according to performances

HOTELS

Hotel OK ($$)

This hulking hotel on 18 floors is centrally located in the heart of Cinelândia. It's popular with business travellers and its rooms and public areas are functional and clean. Some of the staff speak English.

✉ Rua Senador Dantas, 24, Cinelândia ☎ (21) 3479 4500; www.hotelok.com.br

Ibis Rio de Janeiro Centro ($)

Bar-hoppers and business people who want to be close to the centre of the city tend to choose this international chain hotel for its location and good value. Guests can expect modern clean rooms and efficient staff, many of whom speak English. There are excellent transport connections and the nightspots of Lapa are close by.

✉ Rua Silva Jardim 32, Centro ☎ (21) 3511 8200; www.accorhotels.com

Windsor Guanabara Hotel ($$)

This is one of the few good hotels in this part of the city, and is good for those who want to be in the historic centre rather than close to Rio's beaches. It tends to attract business travellers, so expect functional, clean and comfortable rather than luxurious rooms. The staff are friendly, although those working at night don't always speak English. Some of the rooms can be noisy, especially those near the lifts.

✉ Avenida Presidente Vargas 392, Centro ☎ (21) 2195 6000; www.windsorhoteis.com.br

RESTAURANTS

Aipo e Aipim ($)

One of the city's best budget options, with outlets throughout the city, this canteen restaurant offers reasonably priced buffet food and does a brisk trade with office workers. Diners help themselves to dishes from salads and steaks to pasta and sushi, which is charged by weight.

✉ Rua do Ouvidor 108, Centro ☎ (21) 2222 3423 🕒 Mon–Sat 11–6

Atrium ($$$)

Step back in time and lunch in relaxing yet elegant surroundings in this restaurant in the Paço Imperial. Business people and tourists come here to enjoy fine food and fine wines – international and Brazilian.

✉ Praça XV de Novembro 48, Centro ☎ (21) 2220 0193;
www.restauranteatrium.com.br ⏰ Mon–Fri 11:30–3:30

Bar Luiz ($)

Choose from a variety of German dishes, including sausages, potato
salad and sauerkraut. This cosy little bar and restaurant has been a main
player on Rio's downtown scene for over a hundred years.
✉ Rua da Carioca 39, Centro ☎ (21) 2262 6900; www.barluiz.com.br
⏰ Mon–Sat 12–12

Brasserie Rosário ($–$$)

This relaxed, elegant restaurant in an historical house is a lovely spot for
morning coffee, afternoon tea or a light lunch of salad or antipasti. More
indulgent dishes include foie gras, smoked salmon and duck breast.
✉ Rua do Rosário 34, Centro ☎ (21) 2518 3033 ⏰ Mon–Fri 11–9, Sat 11–6

Cais do Oriente ($$)

This restaurant serves Mediterranean food, as well as Oriental and
contemporary cuisine. Diners can eat in one of three areas – on the
pleasant outdoor terrace, inside the sumptuous dining room or on the
intimate mezzanine. The building is late 19th century, beautifully
renovated and filled with antique and rattan furniture.
✉ Rua Visconde de Itaboraí 8, Centro ☎ (21) 2233 2531 ⏰ Tue–Sat 12–12,
Sun–Mon 12–4

Centro Cultural Banco do Brasil ($ and $$–$$$)

The city's best-loved cultural centre is home to two charming eateries
that make a convenient stop-off for visitors taking in the interesting
exhibitions. Choose either the simple, pleasant cafe ($), serving soups,
salads and sandwiches, as well as tea and cake, or the more formal
restaurant ($$–$$$), which offers Brazilian and European favourites.
✉ Rua Primeiro de Março, 66, Centro ☎ (21) 3808 2080 (restaurant), (21) 3808-
2060 (cafe); www.bb.com.br ⏰ Tue–Sun 12–9 (restaurant) Tue–Sun 9–9 (cafe)

Confeitaria Colombo ($$)

Founded in 1894, these historic tea rooms are firmly on the tourist trail,
but well worth a visit. Take tea and cakes in the splendid belle époque

interior and follow in the footsteps of famous Brazilians, from politicians to celebrities. A buffet lunch is served in an upstairs room, but the food is mediocre and overpriced, so stick to drinks and snacks downstairs.

✉ Rua Gonçalves Dias 32, Centro ☎ (21) 2505 1500; www.confeitariacolombo.com.br 🕓 Upstairs daily 11–3; downstairs Mon–Sat 12–3:30

O Navegador ($$)

This buzzing, rather formal, high-ceilinged dining room has been in Rio's Naval Club for more than 30 years. Dishes such as prawns in prosecco and steak with mushroom sauce have a European influence, while offerings such as sun-dried meat, spicy seafood stew and black bean soup are distinctly Brazilian. Light lunches are available at the popular, organic salad bar.

✉ Avenida Rio Branco 180, 6th floor, Centro ☎ (21 2262) 6037
🕓 Mon–Fri 11:30–3

Rio Minho ($)

For more than a hundred years this restaurant has been dishing up traditional Portuguese food. The speciality is *sopa leão veloso*, a tasty Brazilian version of bouillabaisse.

✉ Rua do Ouvidor 10, Centro ☎ (21) 2509-2338 🕓 Mon–Fri 11–4

SHOPPING

Feira Rio Antigo

This monthly market is a lively occasion, as much about enjoying street performers and an al fresco drink at one of the pavement bars, as it is about browsing the street stalls in search of unusual gifts.

✉ Rua do Lavradio, Centro ☎ (21) 2224 6693 🕓 First Sat of the month 10–7

Saara

For an authentic experience away from the tourist shops, visit the vibrant Saara market. Spilling onto the surrounding streets are more than 600 shops selling a dizzying array of items, from Carnaval outfits and artificial flowers to kitchen sinks. Prices are reasonable, but don't be afraid to haggle. Don't carry valuables or large amounts of cash.

✉ Rua da Alfândega and Rua Senhor dos Passos, Centro ☎ (21) 3852 8790
🕓 Mon–Fri 9–6, Sat 9–1

ENTERTAINMENT

Bar Luíz
This is among the best of Rio's *botequims* (traditional bars), many of which are found in this part of the city. Tuck into the high-quality *pestiscos* (bar snacks), an important part of the *botequim* experience.

✉ Rua da Carioca 39, Centro ☎ (21) 2262 6900; www.barluiz.com.br
🕐 Mon–Sat 11–11

Café Amarelinho
Drink in a bit of history, along with the tipple of your choice, at this hundred-year-old *botequim*, which is very popular during happy hour with the after-work crowd. Try the classic bar snack, *bolinhos de bacalhau* (cod balls) and perhaps some delicious *pasteis* (small filled pies) with a cold draught beer.

✉ Praça Floriano 55, Cinelândia ☎ (21) 2240 8434;
www.amarelinhodacinelandia.com.br 🕐 Daily 10am–2am

Centro Cultural Banco do Brasil
Even if you don't go for the culture, the domed, 18th-century building is a lovely place to spend a few hours. This cultural centre, with a popular cafe downstairs and an impressive bookshop, has a lively programme of theatre, cinema, fine art and music. Look out for changing exhibitions on the website or in the local press.

✉ Rua Primeiro de Março 66, Centro ☎ (21) 3808 2020; www.bb.com.br/cultura
🕐 Tue–Sun 10–9

Centro Cultural Carioca
Housed in a beautiful century-old building that is full of atmosphere, this cultural centre with its open veranda attracts talented local names in music and dance. It is an intimate venue with limited seating, so it's best to book ahead.

✉ Rua do Teatro 37, Centro ☎ (21) 2252 6468 or (21) 2242 9642;
www.centroculturalcarioca.com.br 🕐 Box office: Mon–Fri 11–8, Sat 4:30–8:30.
Varying evening opening times depending on performances

Theatro Municipal
See page 88.

Santa Teresa and Lapa

For the many visitors to Rio, Santa Teresa in the cool green hills is a welcome surprise. The pretty neighbourhood has been attracting artists and intellectuals since the 1960s, and in the last decade or so some of the hundred-year-old mansions have been made into boutique hotels.

The historic yellow *bondinho* (little tram) rattles over the whitewashed aqueduct of Arcos da Lapa before making the steep climb up to Santa Teresa. Lapa – also connected to Santa Teresa by a unique, mosaic-tiled staircase, the Escadaria Selarón – is well known for its bars and lively music scene. The tram then clatters up cobbled streets lined with large once-grand houses, hidden behind high walls and wrought-iron gates; the air of faded glamour is palpable. Santa Teresa's main thoroughfare winds past the Museu da Chácara do Céu (Museum in the Sky) and hole-in-wall arts and crafts shops. Spend a pleasant hour or two wandering around the tree-lined streets before visiting one of the lovely neighbourhood restaurants for lunch.

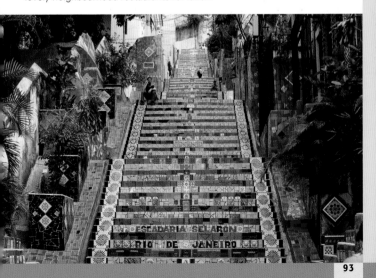

BONDINHO

Rather than walk up the steep hill, take the yellow *bondinho* that leaves from the Estação de Bonde at Rua Lélio Gama 65 near the Carioca metro station. Originally pulled by donkeys, but now electric, it is the last vestige of a public transport system that once served the whole city. The tram is well used and can get very crowded, and you are advised to watch your belongings and not to leave cameras or other expensive items on display. In Santa Teresa, the tram stops at three of the main squares, Largo do Curvelo, Largo dos Guimarães and Largo das Neves.

✚ 9C–7D ✉ Rua Lélio Gama 65, Santa Teresa ☎ (21) 2242 9741 🕘 Daily 6–8 ✋ Inexpensive

LAPA

In the last century, Lapa's nightlife has turned full circle. In the 1920s, its *gafieiras* (dance halls), bars and casinos were filled with the sound of samba and revellers from aristocracy to prostitutes. Following many years of decline, a recent revival has seen it once again become the centre for live music and nightlife. Every weekend sees a popular street party around the base of Los Arcos, with many of the old buildings converted into bars and clubs that are once again filled with live music.

A short walk from the aqueduct is an unusual and delightful staircase, the **Escadaria Selarón.** Chilean artist Jorge Selarón began decorating the 215 steps in 1990 with green, yellow and

blue tiles in homage to the Brazilian flag. Today, most of the tiles that sustain the project are donated – many sent from around the world. Selarón constantly changes the tiles, saying he will finish work on the staircase only when he dies.

✚ 9D

Escadaria Selarón

✉ Rua Joaquim Silva, Lapa to Rua Pinto Martins, Santa Teresa 🕓 Daily 24 hours
✋ Free (donations)

MUSEU DO BONDE

The tiny, one-room Museu do Bonde (Tram Museum) has several hundred objects relating to Santa Teresa's historical tram. Visitors can see original, black-and-white photographs and well-worn conductors' uniforms. Don't miss the still functioning workshop next door, which is home to one of the early trams, and also acts as a graveyard for disused vehicles.

✚ 8E ✉ Rua Carlos Brandt 14, Santa Teresa ☎ (21) 2242 2354 🕓 Daily 10–4
✋ Free

a walk in bohemian Santa Teresa

It's an exhausting, steep walk from Lapa to Santa Teresa (► 54–55), but fortunately a delightful little tram, the Bondinho (► 94) does the hard work. As the rickety yellow streetcar sets off you will see Rio's Metropolitan Cathedral (► 80) on your right, before a dizzying crossing over the white double-arched Arcos da Lapa, an aqueduct that once provided clean water to the city.

On your left you will see the Igreja e Convento de Santa Teresa, the Carmelite convent and church after which the area is named. Casual visitors are not allowed in, but appropriately dressed visitors can attend Mass (Sun 8am).

The tram's first stop is Largo do Curvelo, one of the area's main squares. Stay onboard but take in the surroundings.

Here is Casa Navio (The Ship House), designed to mimic the bridge of a liner. High on the hills above you will also catch a glimpse of Castelo Valentim, which looks like a Bavarian fairy-tale castle.

Next stop is Largo dos Guimarães (► 54–55), the thriving heart of Santa Teresa. Get off the tram here, head down Ladeira do Castro and take the first fork on the left. A few minutes' walk will bring you to the small tram museum.

At the Museu do Bonde (► 95), black-and-white photographs and scale models tell the story of the tram's part in Rio's development.

Stroll back down the street towards Largo do Curvelo.

You will pass open-fronted boutiques selling little hand-crafted models of the *bondinho*, locally made jewellery and paintings depicting local life.

At Curvelo, take the right fork down Rua Dias de Barros, then turn left onto Rua Murtinho Nobre.

Here you will find the Museu da Chácara do Céu (► 98) and the adjacent Parque das Ruínas (► 99), both with good views of the city and bay.

After returning to Curvelo, either continue walking down to Lapa for metro and bus connections, take the tram back into town or grab one of the passing taxis.

Distance 2.5km (1.5 miles)
Time 3 hours
Start point Estação de Bonde, Rua Lélio Gama 65 ✚ 9C
End point Largo do Curvelo ✚ 8E
Lunch Bar do Mineiro ($$; ► 101)

MUSEU CASA DE BENJAMIN CONSTANT

This house museum was, for a short period, home to Benjamin Constant Botelho de Magalhães (1836–91), known as the Founder of the Republic. The restored 19th-century building contains personal items, as well as furniture that belonged to Magalhães. Once part of a large country estate typical of the neighbourhood, the house is surrounded by extensive, tree-filled gardens.

➕ 7E 📧 Rua Monte Alegre 255, Santa Teresa ☎ (21) 2509 1248
🕓 Wed–Sun 1–5pm, gardens daily 8–6 ✋ Free

MUSEU DA CHÁCARA DO CÉU

The Museum in the Sky boasts some impressive works from European artists such as Degas, Seurat and Matisse, as well as pieces by Brazilian artists such as Candido Portinari and Emiliano di Cavalcanti, and a delightful garden designed by Burle Marx. It once belonged to wealthy art patron Raymundo Ottoni de Castro Maya (1894–1968), and visitors can wander the rooms that are still filled with work from his private collection. The library holds an important collection of around 8,000 books relating to art and literature. Finish your visit in the beautifully designed gardens with panoramic views of the city below.

www.museuscastromaya.com.br

➕ 8D 📧 Rua Murtinho Nobre 93, Santa Teresa ☎ (21) 2224 8891
🕓 Wed–Mon 12–5 ✋ Inexpensive

PARQUE DAS RUÍNAS

The Park of the Ruins lies in the gardens attached to the residence of Laurinda Santos Lobo (1878–1946). This well-connected heiress was known for her fabulous parties attended by the city's great and the good, as well as international visitors who happened to be in town, such as Isadora Duncan. The ruins of the house have been fashioned into a modern glass-and-brick structure overlooking the park, which has spectacular views across the city. Cultural events and concerts are held here throughout the year, and there is a small popular open-air cafe.

🕂 8D ✉ Rua Murtinho Nobre 169, Santa Teresa ✉ (21) 2252 1039
🕐 Tue–Sun 8–8

SANTA TERESA, LARGO DOS GUIMARÃES

Best places to see, ➤ 54–55.

HOTELS

Arcos Rio Palace Hotel ($)

This is a basic option and one of the few places to stay in Lapa. It has a plenty of air-conditioned rooms, a small pool and sauna, a bar and 24-hour room service. If you need to find a room at the last minute during Carnaval or major holidays, consider enquiring here; it's a little off the main tourist drag so you may have some luck.

✉ Avenida Mem de Sá 117, Lapa ☎ (21) 2242 8116; www.arcosriopalacehotel.com.br

Cama e Café ($–$$)

This unusual operation provides a central reservation system for bed and breakfast in locals' homes in Santa Teresa. Guests provide a list of requirements and are matched with potential hosts in one of four categories (Economy, Tourist, Superior and Premium Comfort). While it offers a unique opportunity to meet locals, the experience can be a bit hit-and-miss, so approach it with an open mind.

✉ Rua Laurinda Santos Lobo 124, Santa Teresa ☎ (21) 2225 4366; www.camaecafe.com.br

Santa Teresa Hotel ($$$)

This serene and sophisticated luxury boutique hotel is housed in a lovingly restored mansion. Created and managed with regard for the environment, it showcases enchanting Brazilian art in its rooms and communal spaces. The spa, terrace bar and restaurant are among the best in Rio. Opt for a ground-floor room with terrace and hammock overlooking the swimming pool surrounded by tropical gardens.

✉ Rua Almirante Alexandrino 660, Santa Teresa ☎ (21) 3380 0200; www.santa-teresa-hotel.com

Um Meia Tres ($$)

This Santa Teresa hotel may be a bed and breakfast, but it really is a special place to stay. It's homely and friendly, with incredible views across the city, and owners Sue and Bill can't do enough for their guests. There is a 24-hour reception and bar, outdoor swimming pool and air-conditioned rooms with terraces; also free WiFi.

✉ Rua Aprazível 163, Santa Teresa ☎ (21) 2232 0034; www.hotelinrio.net

RESTAURANTS

Aprazível ($$$)

High up in the hills of Santa Teresa surrounded by rainforest, tropical vegetation and exotic flowers is this restaurant in a magical setting. Dine on the terrace with views over the city and Guanabara Bay, or even in the wooden "treehouse". Imaginative Brazilian cuisine is served in a relaxed atmosphere. The *palmitos* (palm hearts) are recommended as a starter – just make sure to leave room for the delicious desserts. A *cachaça* bar and excellent wine list complete the picture.

✉ Rua Aprazível 62, Santa Teresa ☎ (21) 2508 9174; www.aprazivel.com.br
🕐 Tue–Sat 12pm–1am

Bar do Mineiro ($$)

A lovely little neighbourhood bar and restaurant that is *the* spot in Rio for authentic, traditional food from the state of Minas Gerais. Meat and beans feature heavily on the menu and *feijoada* – the national dish of pork and beans – is served all day Saturday. If you don't want to eat, pop in for a perfectly mixed *caipirinha* with *carne seca* (dried meat) and a dish of *pasties* (mini pies) to soak up the alcohol.

✉ Rua Paschoal Carlos Magno 99, Santa Teresa ☎ (21) 2221 9227
🕐 Tue–Sat 11–11, Sun 11–8

Espirito Santa ($$$)

A wide range of Brazilian cuisine, from Amazonian fish and fruits to seafood stews from the northeast is served at this delightful little restaurant with terrace. It's a charming, even romantic spot, although it can get crowded at weekends. The service is good, and the atmosphere relaxed. Don't miss the *caipirinhas* and divine desserts.

✉ Rua Almirante Alexandrino 264, Santa Teresa ☎ (21) 2508 7095
🕐 Mon–Wed 11:30–6, Thu–Sat 11:30am–midnight, Sun 11:30–7

Jasmim Manga ($$)

Pop in for a coffee or fresh juice, or lunch on salad, pizza and Brazilian dishes, with plenty of vegetarian options, at this little cafe with a courtyard. Right in the heart of Santa Teresa, it is one of the few places to offer free internet connection.

✉ Largo dos Guimarães 143, Santa Teresa ☎ (21) 2242 2605 🕐 Daily 9am–10pm

Rio Scenarium ($$)

Steaks, pasta and salads feature on the simple menu of this restaurant, which is also a very popular music venue. Reserve a table, then after dinner continue drinking and dancing. The food is decent, but the music and dancing is particularly special, and if you eat here you get a ringside seat.

✉ Rua do Lavradio 20, Lapa ☎ (21) 3147 9000; www.rioscenarium.com.br
🕐 Tue–Thu 6:30–10pm, Fri–Sat 8–11pm

Sobrenatural ($$$)

Sobrenatural, perhaps Santa Teresa's best-loved restaurant, specializes in fish and seafood. Diners at the rustic-style tables tuck into crab starters, a variety of fresher-than-fresh fish and spicy seafood stews. The large portions are designed to share; just make sure to leave room for one of the delicious desserts.

✉ Rua Almirante Alexandrino 434, Santa Teresa ☎ (21) 2224 1003
🕐 Mon–Sat 12–12, Sun 12–10

SHOPPING

Largo das Letras

This well-stocked bookshop with a small cafe housed in a historic house is a friendly spot that doubles as a local meeting spot. Look out for occasional cultural events, and the flea market held in the gardens on the first Sunday of the month (12–6).

✉ Rua Almirante Alexandrino 501, Largo dos Guimarães, Santa Teresa
☎ (21) 2221 8992; www.largodasletras.com.br 🕐 Tue–Sat 2–10pm, Sun 2–8pm

ENTERTAINMENT

Carioca da Gema

This intimate corner bar in the heart of Lapa is one of the neighbourhood's most enjoyable spots for live music – largely samba and choro. It is also one of the most authentic, continuing to attract a largely local clientele. Even if you don't want to dance, it's a wonderful place to let the professionals and amateurs alike show you how it should be done.

✉ Rua Mem de Sá 79, Lapa ☎ (21) 22210043; www.barcariocadagema.com.br
🕐 Mon–Fri 6pm–1am, Sat 9pm–1am

Guanabara Bay to Tijuca Forest

The winding coast next to Guanabara Bay, where boats bob on the water, is home to a string of low-key neighbourhoods. Although the beaches here are not really suitable for swimming, the stretches of sand make pleasant recreation areas. There are fascinating pockets of history in this part of Rio, with a number of unique little museums, as well as the impressive Museu de Arte Modern (➤ 42–43).

Inland, to the west, is the huge swathe of Tijuca Forest, much of it forming a national park. On the edge of the park, and dominating the hill of Corcovado is the statue of Cristo Redentor (➤ 36–37). No one should miss a visit to this iconic sight, preferably on a clear day for the best views. The park itself, with its cool climate, walks and viewpoints is dotted with historical features and is the perfect location for a scenic drive (➤ 108–109).

CASA DE RUI BARBOSA

Rui Barbosa de Oliveira (1849–1923) was one of the largest figures in Brazilian history. A journalist and judge, he was instrumental in the Abolitionist movement, and twice a Presidential candidate. His pink neoclassical house was opened as Brazil's first house-museum in 1930 and offers a unique insight into domestic life in Brazil at that time. It is surrounded by gardens, one of the few green spaces in the neighbourhood of Botafogo. You can see Rui Barbosa's personal library with 37,000 volumes and wander through the many rooms, filled with more than 1,500 items that belonged to the statesman, including some fine furniture (much of it European), Japanese porcelain and even his 1913 Mercedes Benz car. In the gardens, boulevards and walkways lead past fruit trees and vine-covered pergolas. The house is part of a foundation that carries out research, conservation and education, and is a venue for concerts and theatrical performances throughout the year.
www.casaruibarbosa.gov.br

➕ 20G ✉ Rua São Clemente 134, Botafogo ☎ (21) 3289 4600 ✉ Museum: Tue–Fri 9–5:30. Garden: Mon–Fri 8–6, Sat–Sun 9–6 ✋ Free 🍴 Os Esquilos ($$$; Estrada Barão d'Escragnolle s/n; tel: (21) 2492 2197; Tue–Sun 12–6)

CRISTO REDENTOR

Best places to see, ► 36–37.

MARINA DA GLÓRIA

The compact sweep of this publically owned marina with two floating piers and a sailing school hosts events throughout the year, including Latin America's biggest boat show in April. It is the departure point for cruises around the bay and along the coast, including the **Pink Fleet** cruise ship with restaurant and floating bar. Passengers can enjoy cocktails and lunch or dinner as they sail through Guanabara Bay, past some of the city's most important sites, such as Museu de Arte Moderna (MAM), Praça XV and Ilha Fiscal.

www.marinadagloria.com.br

✚ 10E ✉ Avenida Infante Dom Henrique s/n, Glória ☎ (21) 2555 2200

Pink Fleet

✉ Avenida Infante Dom Henrique s/n loja 2, Flamengo ☎ (21) 2555 4063; www.pinkfleet.com.br ⏰ Fri, buffet dinner and cruise: access to boat 6, tour 9:15–11; Sat, buffet lunch and cruise: access to boat 10:30–11:30, tour 11:45–2:15 💵 Expensive

MUSEU DE ARTE MODERNA

Best places to see, ► 42–43.

MUSEU DO ÍNDIO

The Indian Museum is of huge anthropological significance, and boasts a diverse collection representing Brazil's 270 indigenous groups who together speak more than 180 languages. It is housed in a 19th-century mansion and gardens and also has an important research, educational and preservation role. Permanent exhibitions include audio-visual material, photographs and artefacts in the Museum Village and Indian Art Gallery, and there are activities for children. Changing exhibits may include photographs taken by the Guaraní tribe, or objects relating to the daily life and rituals of the Oiapoque people.

www.museudoindio.org.br

🚩 19G ✉ Rua das Palmeiras 55, Botafogo ☎ (21) 2286 2097 🕐 Tue–Fri 9–5:30, Sat–Sun, holidays 1–5 ✋ Inexpensive (free Sun)

MUSEU DA REPÚBLICA

The engaging Museum of the Republic is housed in the extravagant Palácio do Catete. This was the official and palatial residence of Brazilian presidents from 1897 to 1960 when Rio was the capital. The

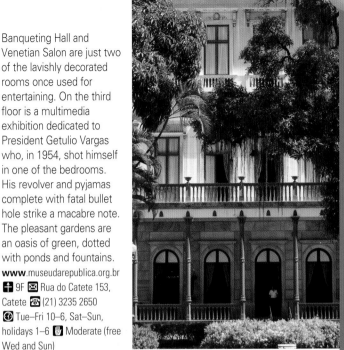

Banqueting Hall and Venetian Salon are just two of the lavishly decorated rooms once used for entertaining. On the third floor is a multimedia exhibition dedicated to President Getulio Vargas who, in 1954, shot himself in one of the bedrooms. His revolver and pyjamas complete with fatal bullet hole strike a macabre note. The pleasant gardens are an oasis of green, dotted with ponds and fountains.

www.museudarepublica.org.br

➕ 9F ✉ Rua do Catete 153, Catete ☎ (21) 3235 2650
🕐 Tue–Fri 10–6, Sat–Sun, holidays 1–6 ✋ Moderate (free Wed and Sun)

MUSEU VILLA-LOBOS

Heitor Villa Lobos (1887–1959) was one of the greatest composers not only of Brazil, but of the Americas, and was responsible for creating around 1,000 works during his career. The 19th-century mansion is filled with pieces relating to his life, including a sound archive, sheet music, personal letters and photographs. You can explore the library and see a short film of his life. Concerts are held in summer in the compact but attractive gardens.

www.museuvillalobos.org.br

➕ 19G ✉ Rua Sorocaba 200, Botafogo ☎ (21) 2226 9818 ✋ Inexpensive
❓ Tours by appointment

PARQUE NACIONAL DA TIJUCA

Best places to see, ➤ 46–47.

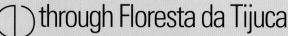

through Floresta da Tijuca

The national park is just one part of the huge Tijuca forest. This drive takes in the park's best waterfall and its highest peak, with hiking and picnic spots along the way.

Begin at the Portão de Entrada, the entrance gate to the national park. Drive 0.5km (0.3 miles) along the Estrada da Cascatinha to the park's most spectacular waterfall.

The Cascatinha do Taunay drops 35m (115ft) and is named after Nicolas Antoine Taunay, a painter who came to Rio as part of the French Artistic Mission.

From the falls, follow the climbing S-bend road for 500m (550yds), then take the fork to the left (Estrada do Imperador) for another 200m (220yds).

On your right, in the dense woods, is Capela Mayrink. This pink chapel formed part of the Boa Vista farm estate and was used by Princess Leopoldina.

Carry on along the road for another 300m (330yds).

Here you will find the Centro dos Visitantes (Praça Afonso Viseu; tel: (21) 2492 2253, daily 8–7). The park's visitor centre can offer safety advice, maps and arrange a guide if required.

Continue up on Estrada do Imperador, taking the second left 350m (380yds) from the visitor centre, and then carry on for another 1.5km (1 mile) to the highest part of the park road.

At 658m (2,159ft), Bom Retiro is a scenic spot for a picnic. If you're feeling energetic, you can do the walk from here to Pico da Tijuca, the highest point of the park, at 1,021m (3,350ft). It takes about an hour to get there on a well-marked trail.

Return the way you came, but take the left fork after 600m (655yds) onto the Estrada Major Archer.

On the right after around 1km (0.6 miles) is Ruínas do Archer, the ruined home of the army officer who led the reforestation of Tijuca.

Continue on for 200m (220yds), then take a right, passing Os Esquilos restaurant after 600m (655yds). After the restaurant, take a right, then a left. From here it is 2km (1.2 miles) back to the park entrance.

Distance 9km (5.6 miles)
Time 3.5 hours
Start/end point Portão de Entrada, Estrada da Cascatinha 850, at Praça Afonso Viseu, Alto da Boa Vista ✚ 13J (off map)
Lunch Os Esquilos restaurant ($$$; ➤ 111)

HOTELS

Caesar Business Rio de Janeiro Botafogo ($$–$$$)

This large, modern hotel is in a central location, close to good transport connections and the shopping centres and with easy access to the beach. One of few upmarket hotels in the area, it tends to attract business travellers, although there is a small pool and leisure centre.

✉ Rua da Passagem 39, Botafogo ☎ (21) 2131 1212; www.caesarbusiness.com

Hotel Paysandú ($)

Although not far from Copacabana beach, this traditional hotel, built in the mid-20th century, is in a quiet area and away from the tourist bustle. It is also among the least expensive options around here. Neither modern nor luxurious, it is comfortable and clean, with a very good breakfast and fast internet connection.

✉ Rua Paissandu 23, Flamengo ☎ (21) 2558 7270

The Maze ($)

This simple, American-owned bed and breakfast in a *favela* (slum) is certainly not for everyone, but it offers a unique experience. All 10 rooms have their own bathroom, there is a kitchen for guest use, and the roof terrace offers panoramic views of Guanabara Bay below. Popular jazz and bossa nova nights are held most Friday evenings and there are regular barbecues and other events.

✉ Rua Tavares Bastos 414, Casa 66, Catete ☎ (21) 2558 5547; www.jazzrio.com

Mercure Rio de Janeiro Botafogo ($$)

An all-suite hotel with rooms that include complete kitchens, which appeals to business travellers as well as families. It may not be close to the beach, but the hotel has good transport connections. Modern rooms and facilities include a pool, jacuzzi, sauna and small restaurant. Look out for special rates that can make this hotel a real bargain.

✉ Rua Sorocaba 305, Botafogo ☎ (21) 2266 9200; www.mercure.com

RESTAURANTS

Laguiole ($$–$$$)

Modern European-Brazilian fusion cuisine is served in a contemporary dining room within the Modern Art Museum. Expect delicate,

accomplished dishes and one of the most impressive wine cellars in the city. A terrace overlooking downtown is open for special events.
✉ Avenida Infante Dom Henrique 85, Parque do Flamengo ☎ (21) 2517 3129; www.mamrio.com.br 🕐 Mon–Fri 12–5

Os Esquilos ($$)

The charming "Squirrel" restaurant, nestled in the rainforest of Tijuca, is housed in a mansion dating from 1850. Sit inside by the fire during winter or outside on the veranda on a warm day. Tuck into traditional Brazilian fare, including the national dish, *feijoada*, on Saturdays.
✉ Estrada Barão d'Escragnolle s/n ☎ (21) 2492 2197; www.osesquilos.com.br 🕐 Tue–Sun 12–6

Pizza Park ($)

Excellent pizzas (more than 30 varieties) are served throughout the day in this friendly restaurant. It's part of a complex with a number of lively bars and restaurants with outdoor tables. Delivery is available too.
✉ Rua Voluntários da Pátria, 446 lojas 18–20, Botafogo ☎ (21) 2537 2602; www.pizzaparkhumaita.com.br 🕐 Daily 11am–midnight

Porcão ($$$)

Arrive hungry at this all-you-can-eat barbecue restaurant and don't let the waiters rush you. Help yourself to salad and sushi and the barbecued meat is brought to your table. This popular chain has a few locations around the city, but this is the best one, with views across to Pão de Açúcar that are particularly impressive around sunset.
✉ Avenida Infante Dom Henrique, Parque do Flamengo ☎ (21) 2554 8535; www.porcao.com.br 🕐 Daily 12–12

Yorubá ($$)

This relaxed and friendly restaurant serves classic Afro-Brazilian dishes, such as *moqueca de peixe* (a spicy fish stew), prawn dishes, including *ebubu fulô* (fish with coconut milk, smoked prawn and banana purée) and some very sweet desserts. It's a little out of the way, so you may want to take a taxi. Early closing times at weekends. Cash only.
✉ Rua Arnaldo Quintela 94, Botafogo ☎ (21) 2541 9387; www.restauranteyoruba.com.br 🕐 Wed–Fri 7–12, Sat–Sun and holidays 12–7

SHOPPING

Loja Artíndia

The Museu do Índio's shop is one of the best places in the city to buy authentic arts and crafts made by Brazil's indigenous people.

✉ Rua das Palmeiras 55, Botafogo ☎ (21) 2286 2097
🕐 Mon–Fri 9–5:30, Sat–Sun and holidays 1–5

São Conrado Fashion Mall

Fashionistas flock to this upmarket shopping centre, which has more than 150 shops selling mostly clothes and accessories. Non-shoppers can retreat to the food court, the multi-screen cinema or the theatre.

✉ Estrada da Gávea 899, São Conrado ☎ (21) 2111 4444; www.scfashionmall. com.br 🕐 Mon–Thu 10–10, Fri–Sat 10am–11pm, Sun 3–9pm

ENTERTAINMENT

Bar do Adão

This local institution has a number of outlets around the city. Join the locals in this heritage house, downing cold beers until the early hours, fuelled by one of the 60 or so different pies they serve here, which some say are the best in Rio.

✉ Rua Dona Mariana 81, Botafogo ☎ (21) 2535 4572; www.bardoadao.com.br
🕐 Mon–Thu 11am–1:30am, Fri–Sat 11am–2:30am, Sun 11–5

Just Fly

Take off from a peak in Tijuca forest, and glide down to a soft landing on São Conrado beach. Just Fly is one of the best operators for hang-gliding in Rio, catering for beginners with tandem flights. Flights depend very much on the weather, so be patient. Cloud permitting, you will be picked up from your hotel and driven up to a ramp in the mountains for "lift off".

☎ (21) 9985 7540 or (21) 2268 0565; www.justfly.com.br ✋ Expensive

Rio Hiking

Hike through Rio's forests and green spaces, go diving or rock climbing or take a trip out to the royal retreat of Petrópolis. They can even arrange nightlife and adventure tours, as well as accommodation.

☎ (21) 2552 9204 or (21) 9721 0594; www..riohiking.com.br ✋ Expensive

Copacabana and Urca

While the magnificent sands of Copacabana Beach are understandably raved about, the neighbourhood of Copacabana has plenty of interest too. It was cut off from the rest of Rio for hundreds of years, until the Túnel Velho (Old Tunnel) opened in 1892 to connect the district with the historic heart of the city, and a few years later, in 1904, the Túnel Novo (New Tunnel) opened. Now, Copacabana is one of the most densely populated areas on the planet, with a huge number of international hotels and apartment blocks, as well as a visible red light district.

Twin forts at either end of the beach highlight the defensive importance of this area in Rio's history, while the central and iconic Copacabana Hotel represents the beginning of its life as a social playground. To the north is the lovely compact neighbourhood of Urca, where the unforgettable Pão de Açúcar is not the only attraction; take the time to enjoy a pleasant waterside walk here, away from the tourist crowds.

AVENIDA ATLÂNTICA

The busy, main road of Avenida Atlântica (car-free on Sundays) runs parallel to the 4km (2.5-mile) crescent beach of Copacabana. Between the sands and the road is the distinctive black-and-white wave-patterned pavement of basalt and limestone, designed by Burle Marx. Fringed by palm trees, the pavement is the site of a touristy night market, Feira Avenida Atlântica (► 123), whose stalls set up around 7pm. Running parallel, one block back from the beach, is the main shopping street of Avenida Nossa Senhora de Copacabana.
✚ 19L–22J

COPACABANA PALACE

This legendary hotel continues to be one of the most prestigious places to stay in the city. Its "Golden" guest book lists politicians, film stars and royalty among its visitors. When it was built in 1923, in the eclectic style, this was one of the few buildings on the beach – look out for pictures of it on evocative old postcards sold in the hotel's gift shop. If the hotel's walls could talk, they would tell tales of Fred Astaire and Ginger Rogers, who danced in a studio model of the hotel in *Flying*

Down to Rio (1933); of Jayne Mansfield, who bared her bosom here during the 1959 Carnaval; and of Orson Welles, who famously threw the entire contents of his hotel room into the pool in 1942. If you don't eat in one of the restaurants here, at least enjoy a cocktail in the bar overlooking the pool.

www.copacabanapalace.com.br

➕ 21J 🖂 Avenida Atlântica 1702, Copacabana ☎ (21) 2545 8790;
🕐 24 hours (poolside bar open daily until midnight)

FORTE DE COPACABANA

The once defensive fort (1914) with its hulking walls is now the Army History Museum. It's a low-key site, but it's worth exploring the battlements for the panoramic view out to sea that stretches from Leme and Pão de Açúcar on one side round to Ipanema on the other. There are changing art exhibitions and military dioramas in the old refectory and sleeping quarters, together with a small souvenir shop. Note that visitors in beachwear will not be admitted.

www.fortedecopacabana.com

➕ 19M 🖂 Avenida Atlântica, Posto 6, Copacabana ☎ (21) 2521 1032;
🕐 Tue–Sun and holidays 10–5 (exhibition), 10–8 (external area) 💷 Inexpensive

a walk around Pão de Açúcar

Hugging the waterfront most of the way, this walk takes you along a rainforest pathway, past a trio of beaches and to the Bay of Botafogo. Explore the charming little neigbourhood of Urca, Rio's smallest, and also its safest, thanks to a large military presence.

Begin at Praia Vermelha, called the "Red Beach", because of its pink-coloured sands. The waters here are not suitable for swimming because of pollution, but it's a lovely spot, backed by a small park.

Hike along the Pista Cláudio Coutinho (daily 6–6), which runs part of the way around Morro da Urca.

This delightful pathway wends it way between the dense mountain forest above and the crashing surf on the rocks below.

Look out for cheeky, capuchin monkeys and colourful butterflies. Paths from here lead up the steep hill to Pão de Açúcar (➤ 44–45); for determined climbers only.

Return to Praia Vermelha and walk 600m (655yds) down grand Avenida Pasteur, and then turn right onto Avenida Portugal.

Small pleasure craft and fishing boats bob in the waters of the sheltered bay of Enseada de Botafogo, with the sands of Praia de Botafogo off to your left across the water.

Follow the waterside path for 1km (0.6 miles), keeping the bay on your left, to the tiny beach of Praia da Urca.

Sugarloaf Mountain looms over the peaceful neighbourhood of Urca, where houses of vastly different architectural styles, many dating from the 1920s, sit side by side.

Stick to the coastal road for another 800m (875yds) to reach Bar Urca (➤ 121), just before the Naval Academy.

Sit on the sea wall and order *petiscos* (snacks) and cold beer as you look over the tranquil bay, with the entrance to Forte São João on your right. It is part of the military area, so is not accessible to visitors.

Distance 3.5km (2 miles)
Time 4 hours
Start point Praia Vermelha 🞤 23H
End point Bar Urca 🞤 23G (off map)
Lunch Bar Urca ($$: ➤ 121)

FORTE DUQUE DE CAXIAS

Named after the Duke of Caxias (1803–80), a key Brazilian military leader and statesman, the fort forms part of a military training area, and is open only during weekends and holidays. The 210m (230yd) walk up to the fortifications is rewarded with superb views over Copacabana beach, across to Urca and out to the ocean as far as Niterói (➤ 164–165). The site of Forte do Vigia (the original "Lookout Fort", built in 1779) is marked by a Brazilian flag. After the Declaration of the Republic, the current fort was reconstructed on the ruins of Vigia and inaugurated in 1919. You can explore the battlements and see the German Krupp cannons that were installed at this time. Since its decommission in 1965, Forte Duque de Caxias has served as an educational and research centre for the Brazilian army.

🔂 23J 🖂 Praça Almirante Júlio de Noronha s/n, Copacabana ☎ (21) 2275 7696 🕐 Sat–Sun and holidays 9–5 💲 Inexpensive

MORRO DO LEME

The Morro do Leme, from which the neighbourhood of Leme takes its name, is the eastern extremity of the Corcovado mountain range, which stretches beyond Parque Nacional da Tijuca. Home to significant numbers of bird and plant species, Leme's green "hill" is part of an environmental protection zone. Partly encircling its base is a pleasant footpath, Caminho dos Pescadores (Fishermens' Walk), which leads through trees next to the waterfront. Note that this trail should not be attempted in rough weather.

🔂 23J

PÃO DE AÇÚCAR

Best places to see, ➤ 44–45.

PRAIA DE COPACABANA

Best places to see, ➤ 50–51.

PRAIA DO LEME

Leme's beach continues where Copacabana's leaves off, the main road of Avenida Princesa Isabel marking the notional division. Just 0.8km (0.5 miles) long, with relatively calm water, and in a mostly residential area, it tends to be much more peaceful than its more famous neighbour, although there are a few international hotels backing it. Praia do Leme mostly attracts locals, including surfers, volleyball players and families. This is one of the only spots in the centre of Rio where Mata Atlântica (the original rainforest) can be seen.

✚ 22J

HOTELS

Augusto's Copacabana Hotel ($)

This is a good-value option, just three blocks from Copacabana beach and with a rooftop pool. Rooms are generally of a decent size, although the hotel could do with some renovation to bring the decor up to date. Some English is spoken by the helpful staff.

✉ Rua Bolívar 119, Copacabana ☎ (21) 2547 1800; www.augustoshotel.com.br

Copacabana Palace ($$$)

See pages 114–115.

Izzy Rent $$

A range of short- to mid-term apartment rentals is available for anything from a single night to several months through this company, which has English-speaking staff. The website lets you search for accommodation, most of which is in Ipanema, Copacabana and Leblon. All apartments have kitchens, air-conditioning and high-speed internet, and a full (uniformed) maid service is available for some apartments. Check carefully what exactly is included in your rental agreement.

✉ Rua General Venancio Flores 187, Leblon ☎ (21) 2522 5768 or (21) 9355 7736; www.ttabrazil.com ⏰ Appointment required

Pestana Rio Atlantica ($$–$$$)

This hotel in the established (Portuguese) Pestana chain occupies a privileged position at the heart of Copacabana's beach road. The spectacular rooftop pool and terrace afford sweeping views of the beach, as do all the beachfront rooms, many with balconies. The hotel attracts business travellers, but it is also a good option for families and couples, especially as free upgrades are often available on check-in.

✉ Avenida Atlântica 2964, Copacabana ☎ (21) 2548 6332; www.pestana.com

Princess Copacabana ($$)

Although this hotel is only two blocks from Copacabana beach, it is significantly cheaper than those on the beachfront. It is an "apart-hotel", where the rooms have kitchens and living areas, as well as bedrooms, making it even better value. All rooms also have a balcony and guests can use the pool with waterfall, fitness centre, steam room and sauna. This is a quiet and clean hotel with helpful staff, although there is no concierge.

✉ Rua Xavier da Silveira 58, Copacabana ☎ (21) 2156 9700; www.promenade.com.br

Sofitel Rio de Janeiro Copacabana ($$$)

All the rooms of this large international hotel, ideally situated at the Ipanema end of Copacabana, have balconies, many of them with sea views. Consider paying a bit more for a Club Millesime room, which includes some welcome extras (full details on website). The hotel has two small pools and full beach service.

✉ Avenida Atlântica 4240, Copacabana ☎ (21) 25251232; www.sofitel.com

RESTAURANTS

Aipo & Aipim ($–$$)

There are a number of branches of this reliable, good-value chain in Copacabana and throughout the city, but this one is centrally located and has something for everyone – from salads to sushi.

✉ Avenida Nossa Senhora de Copacabana 391, Loja B, Copacabana ☎ (21) 2255 6284 🕐 Mon–Fri 11–11, Sat–Sun 11–6

Bar Urca ($$)

This much-loved traditional bar and restaurant overlooking the waters of Guanabara Bay first opened in 1939. Come for a cold beer and a snack of fresh fried sardines, melt-in-the-mouth *empanadas* or something more substantial from its menu, which specializes in Carioca cuisine.

✉ Rua Cândido Gaffrée 205, Urca ☎ 21 2295 8744; www.barurca.com.br
🕐 Mon–Fri 6:30am–11pm, Sat 8am–11pm, Sun 8–8

Café do Forte ($–$$)

This cafe within the fort overlooking Copacabana beach is a lovely spot. Sit in the air-conditioned interior, or on the outdoor terrace, but be prepared to queue at weekends. Breakfast is served from 10am, the salads and pastas are superb, or just pop in for tea and cake. You must pay the entrance fee to the fort (inexpensive) to get into the cafe.

✉ Praça Cel Eugênio Franco 1, Copacabana ☎ (21) 3201 4049;
www.fortedecopacabana.com 🕐 Tue–Sun 10–8

Cervantes ($)

This legendary little place has been going for more than 50 years. It is famed for its meat and pineapple sandwiches, which, along with other snacks, soups and salads, draw people from all over the city. Regular clients sit here for hours, chatting with old friends and drinking *chopp* (draught beer).

✉ Rua Prado Júnior 335, Copacabana ☎ (21) 2295 8744; www.restaurantecervantes.com.br 🕒 Tue–Thu noon–4am, Fri–Sat noon–6am

Cipirani ($$$)

This swish North Italian restaurant within the Copacabana Palace hotel overlooks the swimming pool. Begin with a signature Bellini, then dine on the finest of Italian cuisine, including home-made pasta and bread, all served by attentive waiters. The wine list is excellent. Cipirani tends to attract Rio's elite and gets booked up at weekends. Dress code is smart for both lunch and dinner. Reservations essential.

✉ Avenida Atlântica 1702, Copacabana ☎ (21) 2548 7070; www.copacabanapalace.com.br 🕒 Mon–Sat 12:30–3:30, 7–12

Copa Café ($)

Copa Café is one of Copacabana's best casual eating options. This slick yet relaxed operation is part casual restaurant and part pleasant bar with a small dance floor and very friendly staff. Burgers and salads are the main options on the menu, along with a decent selection of wines and good cocktails.

✉ Avenida Atlântica 3056, Copacabana ☎ (21) 2235 294 🕒 Daily 6pm–1am

Palace Churrascaria ($$)

This fine barebcue meat restaurant in the heart of Copacabana's hotel district also has an impressive salad and sushi bar, and a wide range of seafood. After tucking into your main meal, you won't want to miss out on one of the mouthwatering desserts. Prices here are very reasonable, especially considering the quality, but look for promotions advertised on the site, which offer even greater value for money. Arrive hungry to make the most of this place.

✉ Rua Rodolfo Dantas 16, Copacabana ☎ (21) 2541 5898; www.churrascariapalace.com.br 🕒 Daily 12–12

Le Pré Catelan ($$$)

Within the Sofitel Hotel is one of Rio's finest and priciest restaurants.
Dine on exquisite French-Brazilian fusion cuisine in an elegant setting
with views of Copacabana and the beach. The restaurant has a fine
wine list and offers a 10-course Amazonia menu, which is a real treat.

✉ Avenida Atlântica 4240, Copacabana ☎ (21) 2525 1160;
ww2.leprecatelan.com.br ⏰ Daily 7–11pm

SHOPPING

Elementos da Terra

This lovely little shop sells all kinds of items for the home, fashioned in
wood and other "elements of the earth", such as bamboo and palm
leaves, as well as recycled materials. It is all the work of Brazilian artists,
many of whom work in cooperatives in the interior of the country.

✉ Rua Constante Ramos 61, Copacabana ☎ (21) 2257 0017;
www.elementosdaterra.com.br ⏰ Mon–Sat 10–5

Feira Avenida Atlântica

This nightly street market has been here a long time, but it is aimed
squarely at tourists, so if you do want to buy something, bargain hard.
It's worth a wander through the stalls, which sell souvenirs, bikinis,
sarongs, football tops and jewellery, if you happen to be strolling
through Copacabana during the evening. Do watch your wallet here.

✉ Avenida Atlântica s/n, Copacabana ⏰ Daily 7pm–midnight

MG Bazar

This Aladdin's cave of a shop is filled with Havaianas, Brazilian flip-flops,
of all descriptions. Prices are very competitive here.

✉ Rua Figueiredo Magalhães 414, Copacabana ☎ (21) 2548 1664 ⏰ Mon–Fri
10–6, Sat 10–4

Shopping Cassino Atlântico

Next to the Sofitel Hotel, this air-conditioned shopping centre offers
mostly antiques, art and jewellery. There is also a pet shop, pharmacy
and snack bar. Every Saturday there is an antiques market from 9–7.

✉ Avenida Atlântica 4240, Copacabana ☎ (21) 2523 8709;
www.shoppingcassinoatlantico.com.br ⏰ Mon–Sat 9–9, Sun 2–8

Zona Sul

Supermarkets are a good bet if you are staying in a self-catering apartment, if you want to take a picnic to the beach or even if you want to stock up your mini bar. Zona Sul is one of the most popular chains in Rio, with outlets throughout the city, some which also serve excellent pizzas and breakfasts.

✉ Zona Rua Francisco Sá 35, Copacabana ⏰ Mon–Fri 6:30am–10pm, Sat 6:30am–midnight, Sun 7am–10pm

ENTERTAINMENT

Atlântico

This contemporary, upmarket bar, right in the middle of Copacabana, serves great caipirinhas, as you might expect, as well as food, and also hosts themed nights with DJs throughout the week. Monday is gay night.

✉ Avenida Atlântico 3880, Copacabana ☎ (21) 2513 2485 ⏰ Daily 7pm–3am

Bar do Copa

The historic Copacabana Palace hotel now has a stylish new bar. They may be trying a little too hard with the drop-dead-gorgeous glamour feel, but nevertheless it is a welcome addition to Copacabana's rather tawdry drinking scene. A combination of fibre optics and crystal chandeliers set the scene for cocktail drinking (accompanied by a DJ, Wed–Sat). Be warned: those not staying at the hotel may be greeted by bouncers and a stiff entrance fee.

✉ Avenida Atlântica 1702, Copacabana ☎ (21) 2548 7070; www.copacabanapalace.com.br ⏰ Thu–Sat 9pm–2am

Bip Bip

Locals and visitors come to this very simple bar, little more than a few battered tables, to drink in the atmosphere created by hard-working musicians who specialize in samba and chorinho. They jam together several nights of the week (Tue 9:30pm, Sun 8pm; sometimes other nights) overlooked by the friendly but watchful owner Alfredinho (Little Alfred), who takes his music very seriously.

✉ Rua Almirante Gonçalves 50, Copacabana ☎ No phone ⏰ Irregular opening times but usually Tue–Sun 8pm–1am

Lagoa

Cariocas love their *lagoa* almost as much as their beaches. Here, "Lagoa" refers not just to the large, placid lake of Lagoa Rodrigo de Freitas, but to the neighbourhoods of Lagoa, Jardim Botânico and Gávea, which are clustered around it. These are among the most privileged urban locations on the planet, with mountains, forest, lake and sea all on their doorstep, and they contain some of the most exclusive accommodation in Rio.

The lake and surrounds are a valued leisure area. The water is encircled by a 7.5km (4.5-mile) path, used by joggers, cyclists, families and couples. The simple lakeside kiosks are popular at any time of day, but particularly at dusk. There are plenty of pockets of green in this part of the city, from the tropical enclave of the Jardim Botânico and the huge swathe of Parque da Catacumba to the more manicured spaces of the garden of the Instituto Moreira Salles and Jóquei Clube Brasileiro.

INSTITUTO MOREIRA SALLES (IMS)

Arguably one of Rio's most exquisite cultural centres, the IMS delights on a number of levels. It's in a residential area somewhat off the beaten track, and is a real oasis, with lovely gardens (designed by the great Brazilian landscaper Roberto Burle Marx), complete with swimming pool and fish-filled pond. The IMS was the home of the wealthy Moreira Salles family, who founded and owned Unibanco, one of Brazil's biggest banks; the architecture strikes a typically modernist Brazilian note. On display are changing exhibitions of some of the best in contemporary Brazilian art, from sculpture and paintings to photographs. The institute also holds a valuable archive of material from all fields of the arts, including extensive music recordings, and hosts regular lectures, events and concerts.

http://ims.uol.com.br

✚ 13L (off map) ✉ Rua Marques de Sao Vicente 476, Gávea ☎ (21) 3284 7400; ♨ Free 🍴 Cafe ❓ Tours: Tue–Sat 5pm

JARDIM BOTÂNICO

Best places to see, ➤ 40–41.

JÓQUEI CLUBE BRASILEIRO

Brazil's largest horse-racing track enjoys an envied position between the lake (part of which was reclaimed to make room for the course) and the sea, with Tijuca forest as a backdrop. The elegant site, designed in Louis XV style and inaugurated in 1926, has attracted Rio's elite throughout its long history. Members enjoy exclusive access to the private areas of the Hipódromo da Gávea, as it is also known, with the general public given access for races that are held four times a week. Regular events and concerts are held here, and the horse-racing Grand Prix, which was first held here in 1933, is still a regular August fixture.
www.jcb.com.br

🔲 14K 🖂 Praça Santos Dumont 31, Gávea ☎ (21) 3534 9000 🕓 Races: Fri 5, Sat–Sun 2:45, Mon 6:15; subject to change, check the website for details 💷 Races free (other events expensive) 🍴 Restaurants

PARQUE DA CATACUMBA

The steep slope of the "Catacombs Park" was once the site of a number of *favelas* (slums). These were razed in the 1960s and their 10,000 or so inhabitants forcibly moved out of the city centre. As a way of stopping reoccupation of the area, the powers that be forested the top of the hill and created a sculpture park on the lower section. Walk past the 32 open-air works, by international artists such as Mário Cravo, Bruno Giorgio and Franz Weissmann, and continue up the steep path. You may be lucky enough to see birds and monkeys in the forest, and at the summit there are spectacular views of the city. Unusually for Rio, there are information panels in English.

🔲 17K 🖂 Avenida Epitácio Pessoa 3000, Lagoa ☎ (21) 2521 5540 🕓 Tue–Sun 8–5 💷 Free

PARQUE DA CIDADE AND MUSEU HISTÓRICO DA CIDADE

Rio's City Park is a large, steeply sloping expanse cut through with footpaths and streams. Fountains, once the potable water supply for locals, dot the area, and there are a number of picnic spots. Birds and marmosets can often be seen in the trees. The unassuming **Museu Histórico da Cidade** (City History Museum), housed in a 19th-century mansion that once belonged to a local baron, was created in 1934. Pieces dating back to the founding of the city in 1565 include ceramics, furniture, sculptures, coins and sacred art. There is a permanent exhibition of the key works, with changing displays throughout the year. Next door, the tiny chapel, Capela de São João (Chapel of St John the Baptist), nestling in the trees can normally be visited (ask at the museum). It was built in 1920, and its key feature is a huge mural by Carlos Bastos, a well-known Brazilian artist from the state of Bahia.

www.aamcrj.org

➕ 13L (off map) ✉ Estrada Santa Marinha s/n, Gávea ☎ (21) 2512 2353 or 2294 5990 ⏱ Tue–Fri 10–4. Sun, holidays 10–3 ✋ Inexpensive

PLANETÁRIO

Visitors to the city's modern Planetarium can see thousands of stars projected onto the walls of the enormous Carl Sagan dome (Sat–Sun, holidays 3:30pm, 4:45pm, 6pm; expensive) and explore the **Museu do Universo.** The Universe Museum has permanent exhibitions, with sundials and a copy of the original Foucault's Pendulum, as well as some interesting changing exhibitions and interactive displays.

Four state-of-the-art telescopes in **observation domes** at Praça dos Telescópios (Telescope Square) are preprogrammed to locate more than 60,000 objects in the sky. Sessions are guided by astronomers, who are on hand to answer questions (in Portuguese and English). The Planetarium runs activities and courses and puts on events, such as concerts, throughout the year. Closed during cloudy and rainy weather.
www.planetariodorio.com.br

🞧 13L ✉ Rua Vice-Governador Rubens Berardo 100, Gávea ☎ (21) 2274 0046
Museu do Universo
🕓 Tue–Fri 9–5, Sat–Sun, holidays 3–6 ✋ Moderate
Observation domes
🕓 Tue–Thu 6:30am–7:30pm; summer 7:30am–8:30pm ✋ Moderate

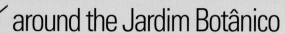

around the Jardim Botânico

Take a walk on the wild side through Rio's lush Botanic Gardens, visiting a peaceful, pretty corner of Japan, an exotic Amazon region and a sweet-smelling sensory garden.

At the entrance, pick up a visitor's guide with a map.

Walk up the Aléia Karl Glasl pathway to the Japanese Garden on your right.

Carp swim in the small pools next to a calming meditation area, surrounded by cherry and bonsai trees.

Continue to the end of Aléia Karl Glasl, crossing two pathways and passing the Rose Garden on your left.

On the right is an enormous pau mulato tree and other tropical plants, including banana trees from the Amazon Region.

Turn left along Aléia Frei Leandro, where you will soon see an old greenhouse on your right.

Inside the hothouse, once used to keep violets, is the Memorial Mestre Valentim. Sculptures of wading birds in bronze and the nymphs Echo and Narcissus, in pewter and lead, honour the Brazilian master craftsman.

Cross over two more pathways and, at the central fountain and a wooden memorial to composer Antonio Carlos Jobim, turn right up Aléia Barbosa Rodrigues.

This is part of the magnificent Avenue of Royal Palms, lined with 137 imperial palms, all descended from the "Mother Palm" planted in 1842, and averaging 25m (82ft) in height and 1m (3.2ft) in diameter.

*Walk through the tunnel of palms
and turn left along Aléia Bento
Pickel, continuing to the junction
with Aléa Frei Velloso and the
Bromelaids Greenhouse.*

Here you will find nearly 2,000
brightly coloured blooms.

*Continue a short distance down
Aléia Frei Velloso to the Orchid
Greenhouse.*

The elegant iron-and glass-structure
is filled with the scent of 3,000
orchids and other exotic flowers,
most of them from Brazil.

*Follow Aléia Alberto Löefgren
as it wriggles around the Lago
Frei Leandro pond, with its 2
m-wide (6.5ft) water lilies. Turn
right onto Aléia J.J. Pizzaro, and
right again onto Aléia Pedro
Gordilho to the end.*

Here is the Sensory Garden and cafe,
from where it is a short walk to the
other entrance at 1008 Rua Jardim
Botânico.

Distance 2km (1.2 miles)
Time 1.5 hours
Start point 920 Rua Jardim Botânico ✚ 14J
End point 1008 Rua Jardim Botânico ✚ 14J
Lunch Café du Lage ($; ➤ 133)

HOTELS

Gávea Tropical ($$$)

At this boutique hotel, with just six luxurious rooms (all with kitchens and balconies with views of the surrounding forest), the owners lavish attention on their guests. It's located in a quiet residential street, not far from the *favela* (slum) of Rocinha. A lovely breakfast is served on the terrace, and there are bicycles for guests to use.

✉ Rua Sérgio Porto 85, Gávea ☎ (21) 2274 6015; www.gaveatropical.com

Lagoa Guest House ($)

This hostel, which has private rooms with shared bathrooms, is in a quiet location within walking distance of the beaches of Leblon and Ipanema. It is very clean, with a jacuzzi and incredibly friendly owners that make it a real home from home. Don't miss the barbecue nights.

✉ Rua do Humaitá 392, Lagoa ☎ (21) 3518 9000; www.lagoaguesthouse.com

La Maison ($$–$$$)

La Maison is a stylish boutique hotel with just five rooms, a pool and terrace, set in lush vegetation and with a view of Cristo Rendentor. Don't expect the pandering service you would get in an international hotel, but the French owner, Jacques, is a great host – drinks and snacks can be had at the hotel and he can advise you on the best restaurants and bars to visit.

✉ Rua Sérgio Porto 58, Gávea ☎ (21) 3205 3585; www.lamaisonario.com

RESTAURANTS

Arab Quiosque ($$)

Everybody's favourite, the "Arab Kiosk" offers a great spread of Syrian and Lebanese dishes, accompanied by plenty of draught beer and live music most nights. Because it's so popular, it can sometimes be hard to get a seat; if so, visit one of the kiosks nearby instead.

✉ Parque dos Patins, Quiosque 7 and 9, Lagoa ☎ (21) 2540 0747 🕐 Daily 9am–last customer leaves

Bar Lagoa ($$)

The art deco building of this bar and restaurant dates back to 1934. The extensive menu has something for every taste, from chicken and fish to pasta and German sausage. Join the locals on the lakeside terrace to watch the setting sun.

✉ Avenida Epitácio Pessoa 1674, Lagoa ☎ (21) 2523 1135; www.barlagoa.com.br
🕐 Mon–Fri 6pm–2am, Sat–Sun noon–2am

Café du Lage ($)

This cafe in the middle of Parque Lage is a delightful spot for a salad, sandwich or coffee and cake. A popular brunch is served at weekends, often accompanied by live music.

✉ Rua Jardim Botânico 414, Jardim Botânico ☎ (21) 9639 9650
🕐 Mon–Thu 9am–10:30pm, Fri–Sun 9–5:30

Mr Lam ($$$)

Prices are comparable to those in the US at this New York export. Diners are treated to a Chinese feast with attentive service at this upmarket restaurant, which is rather conservative in decor and atmosphere. The set menus are a good bet, as is the chicken satay, a speciality. Choose a drink from the extensive cocktail or international wine list, but expect to pay handsomely for it.

✉ Rua Maria Angélica 21, Lagoa ☎ (21) 2286 6661; www.mrlam.com.br
🕐 Mon–Thu 7pm–12:30am, Fri–Sat 7pm–1:30am, Sun 1–11:30pm

Olympe ($$$)

Native Brazilian produce such as tapioca and yams and Amazonian fish are used by the French chef to create elegant fusion dishes, served in a refined setting.

✉ Rua Custódio Serrão 62, Lagoa ☎ (21) 2539 4542; www.claudetroisgros.com.br
🕐 Fri 12–4pm, Mon–Sat 7:30pm–12:30am

Pomodorino ($$)

The contemporary and classic Italian dishes served here are very reasonably priced, as is the wine, especially considering the lovely location. Dine on the large terrace overlooking the lake, or in the grand interior where chandeliers drip from the ceiling.

✉ Avenida Epitácio Pessoa 1104, Lagoa ☎ (21) 3813 2622;
www.pomodorino.com.br 🕐 Mon–Thu 6pm–midnight, Fri–Sat 6pm–1am,
Sun 12–11:30

Roberta Sudbrack ($$$)

The concept of this upmarket restaurant is modern Brazilian food served in multiple small courses as part of a tasting menu. Choices change daily and feature the best of what is in season. Enjoy personal service, with Roberta Sudbrack coming out to greet diners herself. Watch out for expensive drinks; the wine and even mineral water can really bump up the bill.

✉ Rua Lineu de Paula Machado 916, Jardim Botânico ☎ (21) 3874 0139: www.robertasudbrack.com.br ⏱ Tue–Thu 7:30pm–midnight, Fri–Sat 8:30pm–last customer leaves

SHOPPING

O Sol Artesanato Brasileiro

The work of Brazilian artisans from all over the country is sold here. The not-for-profit shop is part of a non-governmental organization that works with local communities and teaches craft techniques to disadvantaged people as a way of increasing their income and promoting traditional handicrafts across the country.

✉ Rua Corcovado 213, Jardim Botânico ☎ (21) 2294 5149; www.artesanato-sol.com.br ⏱ Mon–Sat 10–5

ENTERTAINMENT

Palaphita Kitch

Right on the lake, this is a magical spot at sunset, with views over to Corcovado. There is a spacious outdoor seating area, with sofas as well as tables and chairs. The menu includes a wide range of appetizers, best washed down with draught beer or an exotic fruit *caipirinha* – the drinks of choice for most of the locals who come here.

✉ Avenida Epitácio Pessoa s/n, Quiosque 20, Parque de Cantagalo, Lagoa ☎ (21) 2227 0837; www.palaphitakitch.com.br ⏱ Daily 6pm–2am

Zero Zero

This stylish spot in Gávea plays mostly lounge and electronic music and continues to attract the beautiful crowd. There is a good restaurant, dance floor and a lovely terrace.

✉ Avenida Padre Leonel Franca 240, Gávea ☎ (21) 2540 8041; www.00site.com.br ⏱ Thu–Sun 8pm–4am

Ipanema

Ipanema's sweeping beach is an undisputed world beater, but the neighbourhood itself, with its tree-lined streets and squares and relaxed buzz, has plenty to offer. Intellectuals and artists began to cultivate this area during the 1960s, and, although few real bohemians could afford to live here now, it retains a distinct air of laid-back chic.

Running parallel to the beach, Rua Visconde de Pirajá is the main shopping street, lined with fashion boutiques, book shops and juice bars. Those looking to blow their budget should take a stroll down Rua Garcia d'Ávila, Rio's most sophisticated shopping street, where Louis Vuitton and Mont Blanc can be found.

Forested hills, headlands and look-out points dot the stretch of coast around Ipanema. Here are other lovely, smaller beaches, one of Rio's most interesting *favelas*, and a hang-glider's haunt.

ARPOADOR

Every evening (weather permitting) a crowd gathers at the little headland that divides Ipanema from Copacabana to applaud the sun as it disappears below the watery horizon. Long before the tourists came, whales gathered around the rock, whose name, meaning Harpoon Thrower, is believed to have derived from the hunters who followed them. A small beach on its western side, at Posto 7, has the same name; on the other side is the surfing beach of Praia do Diablo (Devil's Beach), named for its wild waves. Arpoador is overlooked by Parque Garota de Ipanema, a busy park with an outdoor gym, skate-boarding area and children's playground.

✚ 19M

GAROTA DE IPANEMA

Local composers Antonio Carlos (1927–94) and Jobim Vinicius de Moraes (1913–80) are said to have penned the famed bossa nova tune *The Girl From Ipanema* on a napkin in this bar. The story goes that while sipping drinks, they were inspired by a beautiful girl strolling past on her

way to the beach. The walls are covered with reproductions of the score of the song, and while it is touristy, it's a pleasant place for a drink or snack, and perfect for people-watching.

www.garotaipanema.com.br

➕ 17M ✉ Rua Vinicius de Moraes 49A, Ipanema ☎ (21) 2523 3787

🕐 Daily 12–last customer leaves

LEBLON

The canal of Jardim de Ali, which empties into the sea between Posto 10 and Posto 11, marks the end of Ipanema and the beginning of Leblon. This upmarket neighbourhood is one of the most desirable in the city, with apartments in the largely residential area of Upper Leblon regularly changing hands for more than US$1 million. On the leafy side streets of Lower Leblon is a high concentration of cafes and restaurants known as *Baixos* (pronounced "by-shows"). Along the main drag of Ataúlfo de Paiva are boutiques and cinemas, together with bars and nightspots, many of which stay open until the early hours.

➕ 14L

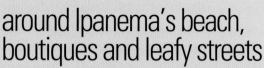

around Ipanema's beach, boutiques and leafy streets

This stroll takes in Ipanema's beach, an historic square and a gem museum, stopping off at two of the city's most well-known bars along the way.

Begin at Posto 10 on Ipanema beach. Walk back from the beach half a block to the art gallery at Rua Mendonça 27.

Established in the 1960s, and still going strong, the Galeria de Arte Ipanema (tel: (21) 2512 8832; www.galeria-ipanema.com; Mon–Fri 10–7, Sat 10–2) showcases the work of some of the biggest names in the Brazilian art world.

Continue for a block and a half, then turn right onto Rua Visconde de Pirajá. Walk one block and turn left down Rua Garcia d'Ávila.

The gem museum, Museu H. Stern (➤ 141), at No. 113, has an adjoining shop and workshop. Short, informative tours are available free throughout the day.

Double back and continue along Visconde de Pirajá, which is lined with interesting boutiques. Another block brings you to Praça Nossa Senhora da Paz, on your left.

This is the site of a farmer's market every Friday morning, selling mostly fresh flowers and vegetables. The square of Our Lady of Peace is named after the church with castellated towers here (Rua Visconde de Pirajá 339; tel: (21) 2241 0003; Mon–Sat 6am–8pm, Sun 6am–10pm).

Continue along Visconde de Pirajá for another block and turn right along Rua Vinicius de Moraes, to the junction with Rua Prudente de Morais.

At No. 49A is the casual corner bar Garota da Ipanema
(➤ 136–137), where the classic bossa nova tune *The Girl from Ipanema* is said to have been written by Antonio Carlos and Jobim Vinicius de Moraes. It's touristy, but a good spot from which to watch the world go by.

Continue down Rua Vinicius de Moraes for another block to the beach.

Just to your right, a huge rainbow flag flies at gay-friendly beach Posto 9. Stop at one of the kiosks here for a refreshing coconut water.

Head along the beach for three blocks, with the sea on your right.

End with a cocktail at the fashionable lounge lobby bar of the chic beachfront Fasano boutique hotel (➤ 146).

Distance 2.4 km (1.5 miles)
Time 2.5 hours
Start point Posto 10, junction of Avenida Vieira Souto with Rua Aníbal de Mendonça ✚ 16M
End point Fasano hotel, Avenida Vieira Souto 80 ✚ 18M
Lunch Forneria São Sebastião ($$; ➤ 148)

MIRANTE DO LEBLON

The look-out point, Mirante do Leblon, at the western end of Leblon beach, offers views over the sands of Leblon and Ipanema, and up towards the hulking Sheraton Hotel and *favela* of Vidigal on Morro Dois Irmãos. There is a small drinks stand here – a locals' haunt – for one last drink and a look out to sea before finally going to bed.

✚ 13M (off map)

MORRO DOIS IRMÃOS

The burning pink sun setting over the Dois Irmãos (Two Brothers) Mountain, named for its twin peaks, is one of Rio's most famous postcard images. The coast road of Avenida Dolphin Moreira leads from the beach of Leblon up the hill, and as it begins to snake around it, it becomes Avenida Niemeyer. Parque do Penhasco Dois Irmãos (daily 8–5) is an attractive, unspoiled area of rare Atlantic rainforest, high up on the hill. It has a play area, trails and several look-out points with views over nearby beaches and inland to Lagoa. The park is best accessed from Aperana Street in Upper Leblon.

✚ 13M (off map)

MUSEU AMSTERDAM SAUER

Showcasing some of the precious finds that followed Mr Sauer's arrival in Brazil in 1940, this museum has informative tours in many languages, and includes a shop. Brazil is responsible for two-thirds of the world's gem production, and more than 3,000 gemstones, such as emeralds, tourmalines and imperial topazes (the latter unique to Brazil) make up the dazzling displays here.

www.amsterdamsauer.com

🕂 16L 🖂 Rua Visconde de Pirajá 484, Ipanema ☎ (21) 2279 6237
🕓 Mon–Fr 9–7:30, Sat 9–4 🖐 Free

MUSEU H. STERN

Semiprecious and precious gemstones and jewellery are on display here. There's an exhibition of uncut precious stones, including topazes, aquamarines and the biggest collection of cut tourmalines in the world, on a workshop tour, then you can visit the shop.

www.hstern.net/hsterninrio

🕂 16M 🖂 Rua Garcia d'Ávila 113, Ipanema ☎ (21) 2106 0000 🕓 Mon–Fri 9–6,
Sat 9–12 🖐 Free

PRAÇA GENERAL OSÓRIO

This square, a block back from the seafront at the Copacabana end of Ipanema is best known for its "Hippie Fair" (► 150) every Sunday, a fixture here since the 1960s. Even if shopping is not your thing, the market is worth visiting to soak up the lively atmosphere, enjoy music and dance performances, and taste some of the snacks from the local street stalls. In the centre of the square is Chafariz das Saracuras (1795), the work of the great Brazilian artist, Mestre Valentim. This fountain, once the focal point of a convent courtyard in the historic centre, was moved here in 1911 when the convent was demolished.

✚ 18M

PRAÇA NOSSA SENHORA DA PAZ

The spacious, green square of "Our Lady of Peace" takes its name from the church opposite. Shady benches dot the well-kept gardens, which include a pond with fountain and a playground. On the corner of the square – bounded by the streets of Rua Visconde de Pirajá and Rua Joana Angélica – fruit, flowers and fish are on sale at a Farmer's Market every Friday morning (6am–1pm).

✚ 17M

PRAIA DO IPANEMA

Best places to see, ► 52–53.

PRAIA DO LEBLON

Leblon's beach is a continuation of the western end of Ipanema beach. The sands here tend to be quieter than the adjoining stretch of Ipanema beach, and the area between Posto 11 and Posto 12 is the location for **Baixo Bebê,** an area dedicated to babies and children up to 10 years old. Parents and nannies with their charges can use the changing room (with free nappies and baby wipes), toys and play area. Attendants hire out beach umbrellas and deck chairs, and paddling pools (which can be filled with fresh water for you, at a price). Don't swim off this beach after heavy rain as the water tends to be polluted.

✚ 14M

Baixo Bebê

✉ Avenida Delfim Moreira, Leblon 🕐 Daily 9–5 ✋ Free

ROCINHA

The *favela* (slum) of Rocinha is one of the largest in Latin America. It is one of 900 in Rio, many of which, like Rochina, are close to exclusive neighbourhoods; in this case Leblon, Rio's equivalent of London's Mayfair. More than a third of the city's population live in these communities, with the daily risk of violence, drugs and police brutality, but most residents are hard-working labourers, shop assistants, nannies and maids.

No one should venture into any of these communities uninvited or unaccompanied. There are well-publicized tours in safari-style jeeps, but many visitors find them a disappointing, zoo-like experience. Such tours might make a token donation to a local school, but provide very little else for the communities and no insight for visitors. Consider a company whose guides live in the community and that demonstrates real commitment to local projects, such as Favela Adventures (http://favelatour.org), which offers a personalized visit to Rocinha on foot.

🚹 13L (off map)

SÃO CONRADO

The 3km (2-mile) beach at São Conrado at the end of Avenida Niemeyer acts as a landing strip for hang-gliders and para-gliders who swoop down onto the sands after taking off from Pedra Bonita in Tijuca. The large swells that often roll into the beach here attract surfers, while children from nearby Rocinha can usually be seen playing on the sands. Behind the beach is the compact and low-key district of São Conrado, dominated by the distinctly upmarket **Gávea Golf Club** (with its golf school) and the huge rock of Pedra de Gávea. Luxury apartment blocks line the streets of São Conrado, which is also home to the huge modern shopping centre, **Fashion Mall.**

🚹 13L (off map)

Gávea Golf Club

✉ Estrada da Gávea 800, São Conrado ☎ (21) 3323 6050; www.gaveagolf.com.br
🕐 Call for opening times 💷 Expensive

Fashion Mall

✉ Estrada da Gávea 899, São Conrado ☎ (21) 2111 4444; www.scfashionmall.com.br 🕐 Mon–Sat 10–10 (restaurants 11–last customer leaves), Sun and holidays 3–9pm (restaurants noon–last customer leaves)

HOTELS

Arpoador Inn ($$)

A very reasonably priced hotel, given that it is right next to the beach between Ipanema and Copacabana, in perhaps one of the best locations in Rio. The basic rooms have scarcely been updated since the hotel was built in the 1970s, but with the sea at your doorstep you probably won't spend very much time inside. Prices for an oceanfront, "luxury" room are around double that for a basic double with no view.

✉ Rua Francisco Otaviano 177, Ipanema ☎ (21) 2523 0060; www.arpoadorinn.com.br

Fasano ($$$)

Ipanema has been in desperate need of a beautiful beachfront hotel like the Fasano for years. Rooms are decorated with lots of Brazilian hard wood with modern, sophisticated touches; it's worth paying extra for a room with a balcony overlooking the beach. Guests can make use of the exquisite rooftop pool and one of the most fashionable bars and restaurants in the city. Be prepared for a certain amount of snobbery.

✉ Avenida Vieira Souto 80, Ipanema ☎ (21) 3202 4000; www.fasano.com.br

Girl from Ipanema ($)

This hostel two blocks back from the beach is one of the cheapest in the area. On offer are both dormitory accommodation and a range of private rooms, some with shared bathrooms. The very helpful staff provide lots of useful local information and there is WiFi and a TV in the communal areas.

✉ Rua Barão da Torre 175, Casa 3, Ipanema ☎ (21) 3507 2165; www.girlfromipanemahostel.com

Ipanema Beach House ($)

For a hostel, Ipanema Beach House offers a high standard of facilities. It even has a small bar, free WiFi and a swimming pool, although prices are a bit higher than a standard option. The accommodation is very basic, even by hostel standards, although most of the sociable guests spend little time in their rooms.

✉ Rua Barão da Torre 485, Ipanema ☎ (21) 3202 2693; www.ipanemabeachhouse.com

Ipanema Plaza ($$$)

This upmarket option in a very central location, opposite Posto 9 on Ipanema beach, has an attractive rooftop area with pool and spectacular views. The quality of service tends to vary, but is generally good. Breakfasts are excellent, but the onsite restaurant is rather average.

✉ Rua Farme de Amoedo 34, Ipanema ☎ (21) 3687 2000; www.ipanemaplaza.com.br

Praia Ipanema ($$–$$$)

A variety of rooms (in some the decor is a little tired) is available at this hotel – choose one on the 10th floor or above for the best views. It's in one of the best locations in the city and, true to its name, right on the *praia* (beach). There's friendly service and a pleasant rooftop pool.

✉ Avenida Vieira Souto 706, Ipanema ☎ (21) 2141 4949; www.praiaipanema.com

Rio Bay Housing ($$–$$$)

Good-quality apartments, studios and lofts with appealing decor (often difficult to find in Rio) are for rent around Ipanema, Leblon and Copacabana, many of them close to the beach. For the price of a three- or four-star hotel room, you will normally get one or possibly two bedrooms, a fully serviced kitchen and sitting room. A five-night minimum stay applies. This multi-lingual, highly professional organization offers a welcome, personal approach.

✉ Rua Nascimento Silva 4C, Ipanema ☎ (21) 8175 6268; www.riobayhousing.com

RESTAURANTS

Bazzar $$

This casual, modern bistro with small outside terrace is a particularly good choice for a snack or lunch. The contemporary menu features light dishes, such as salmon carpaccio and Italian-style tapas, and there's a very decent wine list.

✉ Rua Barão da Torre 538, Ipanema ☎ (21) 3202 2884; www.bazzar.com.br
🕓 Daily noon–1am (Sun to 10pm)

Delírio Tropical $

Pop in for a very reasonably priced buffet-style breakfast or lunch and good people-watching through the large glass windows. Sandwiches and salads, as well as meat and fish dishes, are on the menu at this casual, airy eatery.

✉ Rua Garcia d'Ávila 48, Ipanema ☎ (21) 3201 2977; www.delirio.com.br
🕓 Mon–Sat 9am–10pm, Sun and holidays 9–9

Forneria São Sebastião $$

This stand outs in Ipanema as the perfect lunch spot. It has all you would expect from a modern Italian menu, from melt-in-the-mouth, thin-crust pizzas, a good selection of antipasti, prawn risotto and calamari salad, and a killer cashew Martini. Although some locals come to this sophisticated bar and restaurant to be seen, it avoids pretentiousness, with slick yet friendly service.

✉ Rua Aníbal de Mendonça 112, Ipanema ☎ (21) 2540 8045; www.forneria.com.br 🕓 Mon–Thu noon–1am, Fri–Sat noon–2am

Frontera ($)

Frontera is a popular and relatively upmarket *comida por quilo* (food by weight) restaurant that gets particularly busy at lunch time. A huge variety of buffet food is on offer, from sushi and salad to Portuguese and Italian specialities.

✉ Rua Visconde de Pirajá 128, Ipanema ☎ (21) 3289 2350; www.frontera.com.br
🕓 Daily 10am–11pm

Gero ($$$)

An import from the city of São Paulo and part of the Fasano hotel and restaurant stable, Gero offers Italian fine dining, with all the classics, a good, if rather over-priced wine list, and impeccable service. A strict dress code is in place at this restaurant that prides itself on attracting Brazilian celebrities and high society. Can be rather pretentious.

✉ Rua Aníbal de Mendonça 157, Ipanema ☎ (21) 2239 8158; www.fasano.com.br
🕓 Sun–Th 12–4, 7–1, Fri 12–4, Sat 12–2

Gula Gula ($–$$)

This atmospheric, casual cafe and restaurant occupies an historic villa in Ipanema and has long been a favourite with locals. Gula Gula is spreading fast as a franchise, with locations throughout the city, many of them in shopping centres. It excels as a lunch spot: the quiche and salads come highly recommended, but there is a good range of Brazilian food too, including steaks, as well as good desserts and cakes.

✉ Rua Henrique Dumont 57, Ipanema ☎ (21) 2259 3084; www.gulagula.com.br
🕐 Sun–Thu 12–12, Fri–Sat noon–1am

New Natural Restaurant ($)

Good-value, tasty salads, pasta, vegetable and meat dishes can all be eaten in or taken away at this neighbourhood *comida por quilo* (food by weight) restaurant. Fresh juices and coconut water are for sale too. There is a health food shop attached.

✉ Rua Barão da Torre 173, Ipanema ☎ (21) 2287 0301 🕐 Daily 8am–11pm

Sorvete Italia ($)

Delicious cooling ice creams and sorbets are on sale here in all kinds of flavours, from Amazonian fruits to rich chocolate. If that all sounds too indulgent, there are diet versions and yoghurt desserts.

✉ Avenida Visconde de Pirajá 187, Ipanema ☎ (21) 2256 6139;
www.sorveteitalia.com 🕐 Daily 9–9

Sushi Leblon ($$$)

This is probably the best Japanese restaurant in Rio, although the food doesn't come cheap. There is fresher-than-fresh sushi and sashimi, of course, but also plenty of cooked fish and noodle dishes. It's a stylish spot, where locals come to be seen as much as to eat, and it gets very crowded from around 9pm, when a hostess appears on the door. Bookings are essential in the evenings.

✉ Rua Dias Ferreira 256, Leblon ☎ (21) 2512 7830; www.sushileblon.com
🕐 Mon–Fri 12–4, 7–12, Sat noon–1am, Sun 1:30pm–midnight

Za Zá ($$)

This funky bar and restaurant on three floors has a small, fairy light-covered terrace. On the top floor, diners remove their shoes and sit on large cushions on low tables, Japanese style. The truly eclectic menu has everything from sushi and seafood noodles to Moroccan pastilla and spicy samosas. Don't miss the delicious desserts and cocktails.

✉ Rua Joana Angélica 40, Ipanema ☎ (21) 2247 9101; www.zazabistro.com.br
🕐 Daily 7pm–1am

SHOPPING

BumBum

Founded in 1979, this is one of the best places to purchase a Brazilian bikini. BumBum has outlets throughout the city, but this is probably the most well known. You can mix styles, colours and sizes of bikini bottoms and tops, and the assistants are always helpful. They also sell bathing suits for men.

✉ Rua Visconde de Pirajá 351, Ipanema ☎ (21) 3259 8630 🕓 Mon–Sat 9–8

Feira de Artesanato de Ipanema

Everyone knows the Handicrafts & Art Fair of Ipanema as the "Hippie Fair". It's a fun, if touristy event selling everything from local art and leather beanbags to home-made cakes and stuffed piranhas.

✉ Praça General Osório, Ipanema 🕓 Sun 7–7

Gilson Martins

This is the main outlet of one of Brazil's most famous designers and a local institution that has been joined by a second shop in Copacabana. On sale are funky bags and purses decorated with Rio icons such as Corcovado and Cristo Redentor, as well as the Brazilian flag.

✉ Rua Visconde de Pirajá 462, Ipanema ☎ (21) 2227 6178; www.gilsonmartins.com.br 🕓 Mon–Sat 9–8, Sun 2–8pm

Livraria da Travessa

This small chain has seven *livrarias* (bookshops) in Rio. The shops are little havens where you can browse books, including English-language titles and international magazines, and listen to CDs. Most of the shops have cafes, so you can do all this while enjoying a coffee.

✉ Rua Visconde de Pirajá 572, Ipanema ☎ (21) 3205 9002; www.travessa.com.br 🕓 Mon–Sat 9am–midnight, Sun 11am–midnight

Toca do Vinicius

This charming little neighbourhood music shop run by its friendly owner sells a variety of music and books related to bossa nova. It hosts small concerts on the pavement and there is a bijoux gallery upstairs.

✉ Rua Vinicius de Moraes 129, Ipanema ☎ (21) 2247 5227; www.tocadovinicius.com.br 🕓 Mon–Sat 9–9, Sun 10–5 (until 9pm on Sun if there is an event)

ENTERTAINMENT

Academia da Cachaça
This tiny bar and shop is the Holy Grail for *cachaça* lovers, offering more than a hundred different brands.
✉ Rua Conde Bernardotte 26, Leblon ☎ (21) 2492 1159;
www.academiadacachaca.com.br ⊙ Mon–Thu 12–8, Fri–Sun 12–9

Bar Bofetada
Bar Bofetada is well known as a gay and lesbian friendly spot and is particularly popular as a pit stop after a day at the beach.
✉ Rua Farme de Amoedo 87, Ipanema ☎ (21) 2227 1675 ⊙ Mon–Sat 8am–2am, Sun 8am–1am

Dama de Ferro
This club has been one of the coolest around for several years. Gay and lesbian friendly, it also attracts large numbers of straight people.
✉ Rua Vinicius de Moraes 288, Ipanema ☎ (21) 2247 2330;
www.damadeferro.com.br ⊙ Fri–Sun 11pm–5am

Devassa
The city's own microbrewery serves Guinness and beer to a discerning crowd in locations around the city, including this bar in Leblon.
✉ Avenida General San Martin 1241, Leblon ☎ (21) 2540 6087;
www.devassa.com.br ⊙ Mon–Fri 5pm–last customers leaves, Sat–Sun 2pm–4am

Lord Jim Pub
Should you find yourself hankering after a British-style pub, the Lord Jim serves up classic British dishes, such as steak and kidney pie, malt whiskies, draught Guinness and Newcastle brown ale.
✉ Rua Paul Redfern 63, Ipanema ☎ (21) 2249 4881; www.lordjimpub.com.br
⊙ Mon–Thu 6pm–2am, Fri 6pm–4am, Sat–Sun 2pm–4am

Vinicius Piano Bar
A long-standing "show bar" and restaurant where you can listen to live bossa nova performed by some of Brazil's best artists.
✉ Rua Vinicius de Moraes 39, Ipanema ☎ (21) 2523 4757;
www.viniciusbar.com.br ⊙ Daily 9pm–4am

Excursions

Angra dos Reis	155
Búzios	156–159
Ilha Grande	160–163
Niterói	164–165
Paraty	166–169
Petrópolis	170–171
Praias de Zona Oeste	172–175
Teresópolis	176–177

Beyond Rio's beautiful city beaches are some unspoiled, and often deserted, stretches of sand to the west. It is well worth spending a day exploring these outlying beaches, either visiting all of them, or perhaps just one or two, combined with lunch at one of the area's seafood restaurants overlooking the sea.

Travel further west to Rio State and the start of the spectacular, aptly named Costa Verde (Green Coast), where a thick strip of Atlantic forest tumbles down to the turquoise ocean below. Just a few hours from Rio de Janeiro is the desert island retreat of Ilha Grande, where the pace of life is so relaxed you could be in another world. Spend your days on the empty sand beaches, hiking in the lush jungle or kayaking in the clear water. A few hours further west is the charming colonial town of Paraty, with its own pretty beaches, whose cobbled streets resonate with history.

East takes you to the city of Niterói, with its architectural trail and the sophisticated resort of Búzios; north is the historic green retreat of Petrópolis and the hiking base of Teresópolis.

ANGRA DOS REIS

The "Cove of Kings" lies 170km (110 miles) from Rio de Janeiro. Its 365 islands and 2,000 beaches make it a popular weekend and holiday retreat; many Brazilian celebrities have vacation homes here, and most of the large hotels and resorts are five star.

The unassuming little town acts as the gateway to the beaches, many of them on islands in the bay. Most of Angra dos Reis' beaches can be reached only by boat, but a good number, including the attractive Bonfim and Gordas beaches, can be easily accessed from the Estrada do Contorno road. The coast here is dotted with sailing clubs and marinas and its clear waters are filled with tropical fish and underwater wrecks, making for some of the best diving in Brazil. The excellent visibility means you can see a lot with just a snorkel.

Angra dos Reis is backed by the lush Serra do Mar mountain range, a scenic inland area of forests, rivers and waterfalls that can be explored on foot, horseback or by jeep. The Mambucaba River offers exciting kayaking and rafting trips.

BÚZIOS

Relaxing on one of the many beaches, dining in sophisticated restaurants and promenading along Rua das Pedras (Street of Stones) are the main activities on Búzios, 170km (106 miles) east of Rio. This peninsula has long been a playground for international celebrities and wealthy Brazilians, but now attracts visitors from around the world. Many return year after year and it gets very crowded during summer (between December and February).

Beaches

The slender 8km (5-mile) peninsula has 25 beaches, all of which can be reached on day trips. Some stretches of sand have shallow pools offshore, which are ideal for children, other bigger beaches are fashionable hangouts, and for those who really want to get away from it all, there are hidden coves once used by pirates. These include the twin beaches of Azeda and Azedinha, a half-hour walk from the beach at Ossos, and now part of an environmental protection zone.

The 4km (2.5-mile) expanse of Praia da Geribá, lined with restaurants, is one of the most popular beaches. Families flock to the beach of

Praia da Ferradurinha (Little Horseshoe), which has sheltered sands and waters. Snorkelling is particularly good in the coral-filled, clear waters of Praia de João Fernandes and Praia Tartaruga, which are also both good dive spots. Unspoiled and often nearly empty, Praia dos Amores (Lovers' Beach) and neighbouring Praia das Virgens are unofficial nudist beaches, reached only by scrambling along the rocks or by boat.

Communities

There are three main settlements on the peninsula. Ossos, largely removed from the tourism industry retains much of its original character. Manguinhos is rather unattractive, although its beach with

nearly constant calm waters and consistent winds is a prime
windsurfing spot, along with neighbouring Formosa Bay. Armação de
Búzios is the "capital". Here, Rua das Pedras (Street of Stones) is a
cobbled, pedestrianized street just 500m (550yds) long, lined with
shops and restaurants. Orla Bardot, at the eastern end of Rua das
Pedras, is a pretty promenade next to the water. It is named after
Búzios' most famous patron, Brigitte Bardot, who visited in 1964
and made the beach resort world famous.

Activities

Sporting types will find plenty to occupy themselves on Búzios. Surfing,
diving and snorkelling are popular and easily arranged. Travelling around
the peninsula is by boat, bike, car, taxi, beach buggy or simply on foot.
Boat tours leave for the beaches from Pier do Centro every morning.
Choose from battered fishing boats, slick schooners, functional dive
boats and fast water taxis. Isla Feia (Ugly Island) is perhaps one of the
best diving spots in the whole area. Visibility is good year-round, and if
you don't want to take to the deep, try one of the snorkelling trips
instead. Youngsters love the glass-bottomed catamarans that offer a
window on the fish-filled natural aquarium below the surface.

Nature reserves

Away from the beach, hikers and nature lovers can enjoy a visit to one of the nature reserves within the peninsula's Atlantic forest, filled with hundreds of species of butterflies, birds and flowers and endangered golden tamarind monkeys. The **Reserva Tauá** is a private initiative that has been hugely successful in restoring the original habitat of the area. It is thought to contain a staggering 40 per cent of the 1,300 species of bromeliads found in Brazil. Guided tours can be arranged by contacting the website (www.reservataua.com.br) in advance. The **Instituto Ecológico Búzios Mata Atlântica** (Buzios Atlantic Forest Ecological Institute) organizes walks through the Atlantic forest of Emerências Reserve on Monday, Wednesday and Friday.

Reserva Tauá

✉ 2.5km (1.5 miles) from Alto da Rasa (on dirt road), Vila Verde ⏰ Daily 8–6

Instituto Ecológico Búzios Mata Atlântica (IEBMA)

✉ Estrada Velha de Búzios (Old Búzios Road) Km 5 ☎ (22) 2623 2200 ❓ Walks last approximately one hour

Búzios Golf

Búzios Golf is an international standard, 18-hole golf course with seven reasonably priced practice greens. Beautifully located in a valley, with dense vegetation and scenic lakes, it is widely regarded as one of the best golf courses in Brazil. On site is a golf resort with accommodation, as well as a show-jumping club.

✉ Marina Porto ☎ (22) 2629 1240; www.buziosgolf.com.br ✋ Expensive

ILHA GRANDE

Closed off from the world until 1994, Ilha Grande (Big Island) is 150km (93 miles) south of Rio and 20km (12 miles) from the mainland. It retains something of a desert island feel; there are no roads or cars and everyone gets around on foot or by boat. Visitors come here to get away from it all, hike along pretty trails through the lush vegetation filled with monkeys and exotic birds, or kayak in the clear water.

Island protection

Strict building restrictions mean the only hotels are rustic *pousadas* (small inns) or little resort hotels. The delicate ecosystem of both the land and surrounding waters are part of an environmental protection zone, protected by law, and much of Ilha Grande and its beaches are completely undeveloped. The whole island is carpeted in rare Mata Atlântica (Atlantic forest) and surrounded by calm, green waters.

Ilha Grande has a rich and fascinating history. Before the arrival of Portuguese explorers in the 16th century, 150 or so native Indians led a simple, peaceful life here, hunting and fishing. Between the 16th and 18th centuries, the hidden coves of this isolated island were a haven for European pirates, plundering the Portuguese and Spanish ships that transported gold back from the colonies. Later, slave ships hid here, attempting to circumvent the ban on their trade. Well into the 20th century, a leper hospital functioned on the island, and for most of that century it was also a Brazilian prison, like Alcatraz. It was here that the military dictatorship locked away anyone who dared criticize the regime, as well as some legitimate dangerous criminals.

Praia Lopes Mendes

More than a hundred beaches with fine white sand fringe the island, including the magnificent 3km (2-mile) long Praia Lopes Mendes. Backed by Atlantic forest, it is regularly voted one of the most beautiful beaches in the world. There is no development or kiosks here, so bring your own food and drink, as well as sun protection, as there is very little shade. Lopes Mendes can be reached by return boat trip from Vila do Abraão, followed by a steep 20-minute walk; alternatively you can walk the three hours from the village, then take the boat back. Consistent good breaks on this large sweep of beach, and shallow water for a long

way from the shore mean surfing is popular here, and boards and lessons are available. Offshore is the tiny island of Jorge Greco (Greek George), which is rumoured to be named after a Greek pirate who once made his home here. It is possible to swim (if you are confident), or take a boat out to the island, which has its own lovely little beach.

Pico do Papagaio

Inland are scenic waterfalls, clear rivers, blue lagoons and Pico do Papagaio (959m/3,146ft). "Parrot's Peak", which is named because of its beak-like shape, can be scaled in three hours, offering bird's-eye views of the beautiful island and across the water to the mainland. The trail to the top is not clearly marked, so a guide (who can be hired in the village) is highly recommended. Most of the other trails here (and there are many criss-crossing the island) are well signposted, and range from easy to difficult. Nonetheless, it is advisable to hire a guide, not only for safety but because they can provide information about the surrounding landscape, plants and wildlife. Committed hikers circumnavigate the whole island, following a coastal footpath, which takes about a week. Bear in mind that accommodation and food supplies are not easily found along most of this route.

Vila do Abraão

The island "capital" of Vila do Abraão is a tiny settlement – little more than a few sand and cobbled streets with the occasional bar/restaurant and several small boutiques and souvenir shops (there are no supermarkets). Vila, as it is usually known, has a handful of tour agencies that offer trips around the island. Most operators are on the the main road of Rua da Praia (Beach Street). There are two piers in Vila do Abraão; the one to the east is where ferries arrive from and leave for the mainland, while the pier further west is where boat trips around the island depart. The murky waters here are not suitable for swimming due to pollution from the ferries and other vessels.

NITERÓI

Although often regarded as a suburb of Rio, Niterói is a city in its own right. You can reach it by taxi, or by bus from Praça XV in the Centro Histórico (➤ 48–49) crossing the 13km (8-mile) Rio–Niterói bridge. Alternatively, hop on one of the frequent ferries from Praça XV, which take 20 minutes, or a hydrofoil or catamaran (just 5 minutes).

Niterói's bay beaches, while popular, are not recommended for swimming. Icaraí – Niterói's answer to Copacabana – is the largest and most popular stretch of sand. Nearby Charitas is a good spot for water sports. For an altogether more pleasant backdrop, head out to the ocean beaches, the closest of which is Piratininga, with good views of Rio's Sugarloaf. Pretty Praia de Itaipu, backed by dunes, is home to a small fishing community. The last of this group of beaches is Itacoatiara, which is well worth the journey, with green mountains plunging down to the sea.

Fortaleza de Santa Cruz da Barra

This sprawling defensive fort was built on a promontory at the eastern end of the bay. In 1555, the French built a simple construction (with just two cannons), which was progressively enlarged until the middle of the 18th century to form the hulking defensive structure it is today. The undisputed highlight is the spectacular view from the look-out point of Mirante do Pontal.

✉ Estrada General Eurico Gaspar Dutra s/n, Jurujuba ☎ (21) 2710 7840
🕐 Tue–Sun 10–5 🍴 Cafe ($) and gift shop ❓ Entry by 45-minute guided tour only

Museu de Arte Contemporanea

The Contemporary Art Museum (MAC), with its sweeping views and unique design by legendary Brazilian architect Oscar Niemeyer, is undoubtedly the star attraction here, although the art itself is rather uninspiring.

www.macniteroi.com.br

✉ Mirante da Boa Viagem ☎ (21) 2620 2400; 🕐 Tue–Sun 10–6 (7pm summer weekends); last admission 15 mins before closing. External courtyard 9–7 (Sat–Sun 9–8) 💰 Inexpensive

PARATY

On the aptly named Costa Verde (Green Coast), some 240km (150 miles) south of Rio, Paraty (also spelt Parati) is a charming, colonial town with cobbled streets, where family-run *pousadas* and souvenir shops operate in restored 19th-century houses. Cars are prohibited from the centre, and the donkeys and carts used for transport add to the old-world feel. You can wander the pedestrianized, cobblestoned compact historical centre, visiting the boutiques, restaurants and cultural centres that have breathed new life into the attractive colonial houses. Rickety old fishing boats, state-of-the-art schooners and modern catamarans at the pier offer competing island-hops around the bay, a trip not to be missed.

Paraty was once Brazil's second biggest port and one of its richest cities. During the early 1800s, gold, diamonds and other gems extracted from Minas Gerais were transported on the backs of slaves and donkeys through the Serra do Mar mountain range and shipped back to Portugal. They used trails that had been hewn by hand by the original inhabitants of Paraty, the Guaianás, who named the settlement after a local fish. Paraty became the last stop on the important route known as the Caminho do Ouro, the Gold Trail.

When an alternative route between Rio and São Paulo was built, Paraty and its splendid colonial houses that had been built at the time were largely forgotten. By the end of the 18th century, several hundred farms and distilleries were producing sugar and *cachaça*, which were sold on the international market. The quality of the *cachaça* here was so good that Paraty became synonymous with the famous sugar-cane spirit.

The town's fortunes were further revived during the coffee boom of the mid-19th century, but the abolition of slavery in 1888 sounded another death knell for Paraty's topsy-turvy prosperity. It wasn't until the town was declared part of Brazilian Historical Heritage in 1966, and the main Rio–Santos road was built in the 1970s, that Paraty once again began to receive any kind of real attention. This time it was from tourists, who began flocking to the beautifully preserved colonial town.

Caminho do Ouro

The Caminho do Ouro (Gold Trail) begins 9km (5.6 miles) outside Paraty on the Paraty–Cunha Road within the lush Parque Nacional Serra da Bocaina. Gold and gemstones once poured down this deep vein that leads through the steep wall of the Serra do Mar mountain range, swathed in Atlantic forest. Two kilometres (1.2 miles) of the 1,200km (746-mile) walkway have been cleared and restored and can be walked on tours that include cooling dips in the clear waterfalls and a visit to a *cachaça* distillery. Any of the agencies in town can provide further information and arrange walking tours, as well as trips by bike, jeep, horse and kayak.

www.caminhodoouro.com.br

✉ Rua Dona Geralda 327 ☎ (24) 3371 1575; 🕐 Wed–Sun 9–5 ✋ Expensive

Casa da Cultura

On entering the House of Culture, visitors walk over a carpet of coloured sawdust that is typical of the local religious folk art and into the Sala da Cultura Índigena (Room of Indigenous Culture), dedicated to the Guaianás, who were the original inhabitants of the bay. The second floor contains a permanent exhibition of art and everyday objects relating to the people who live in the area, while a peaceful courtyard hosts multimedia and temporary exhibitions, some of them interactive.

www.casadaculturaparaty.org.br

✉ Rua Dona Geralda 177 ☎ (24) 3371 2325; 🕐 Wed–Mon 10–6:30 ✋ Inexpensive

Colonial Churches

Paraty has a high concentration of churches, but the splendid baroque **Igreja de Santa Rita** (1722) is its most impressive, and one of the town's enduring images, in an imposing position near the pier. The church's simple exterior belies the ornately decorated interior, which contains a small museum of sacred art, the Museu de Arte Sacra. The more austere **Igreja de Nossa Senhora do Rosário** (1725), which was built by and for slaves, features some gold leaf, but that was added in the 20th century.

Igreja de Santa Rita

✉ Largo Rosário ⏱ Wed–Sun 10–12, 2–5 ✋ Free

Igreja de Nossa Senhora do Rosário

✉ Rua do Comércio/Rua Samuel Costa ⏱ Wed–Sun 9–12, 1:30–5 ✋ Free

Trindade

Once a little hippy colony with a few fishermen, Trindade may now be firmly on the tourist map, with campsites, houses to rent and an increasing number of *pousadas*, but it is still delightfully tranquil, with a variety of unspoiled beaches to explore. It lies 25km (15 miles) from Paraty and is a 40-minute bus ride, or a half-hour by taxi.

PETRÓPOLIS

The summer retreat of the Portuguese royal family in the cool green hills 72km (45 miles) north of Rio is an hour away by car or bus. Consider staying overnight in one of its charming *pousadas*, but avoid visiting on Monday, when many of the attractions are closed.

Museu Imperial

The pink neoclassical palace that is now the Imperial Museum was once the summer residence of King Pedro II and his wife. Visitors must don felt slippers to protect the sheen of the white Carrara and black Belgian marble floor of the entrance hall, then can wander around the different rooms filled with fine mahogany furniture and personal effects, from jewellery to paintings. Dom Pedro II's diamond- and pearl-studded gold crown is a highlight. From outside the museum, horse-drawn carriages offer a variety of circuits around the town (daily 8–5).
www.museuimperial.gov.br

✉ Rua da Imperatriz 220 ☎ (24) 2237 8000; 🕔 Tue–Sun 11–6 💷 Moderate
🍴 Cafe, restaurant ❓ Sound and light show (Thu–Sat 8pm, expensive)

Catedral de São Pedro de Alcântara

The 70m-high (230ft) tower of the neo-Gothic Catedral de São Pedro de Alcântara, which dates from 1884, rises above the mostly 19th-century buildings of Petrópolis.

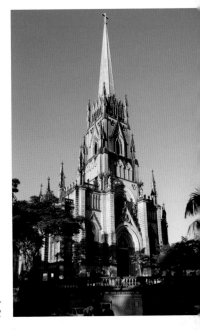

✉ Rua São Pedro de Alcântara 60
☎ (24) 2242 4300 🕐 Mon–Sat 8–noon, Tue–Sat 2–6, Sun 8–1, 3–6 ✋ Free

Casa de Santos Dumont

Santos Dumont, the Brazilian father of aviation, called his Petrópolis summer house A Encantada (The Enchanted One), and Casa de Santos Dumont, filled with a fascinating collection of quirky inventions, really is a delight.

✉ Rua do Encanto 22 ☎ (24) 2247 5222
🕐 Tue–Sun 9:30–5 ✋ Inexpensive

Casa da Ipiranga

The house and gardens of Casa da Ipiranga date from 1884 and can be visited on a guided tour, or during one of the music concerts hosted there. The hundred-year-old stables house a restaurant and wine cellar, as well as Petrópolis's first clock tower.

✉ Rua Ipiranga 716 ☎ (24) 2231 8718 🕐 Thu–Tue 10–6 ✋ Inexpensive
❓ Guided visits: Praça Expedicionários s/n, tel: (24) 2246 9377; www.petropolis.rj.gov.br; Mon–Sat 9–6, Sun 9–5

Casa do Barão de Mauá

The Casa do Barão de Mauá, the home of the great industrialist Baron Mauá, today houses the Petrópolis Foundation for Culture and Tourism. For a glimpse inside visit reception during office hours.

✉ Avenida Barão do Rio/Avenida Piabanha 🕐 Mon–Fri 9–5 ✋ Free

PRAIAS DE ZONA OESTE

The Beaches of the West Zone make for an enjoyable day trip from Rio, including a couple of hours driving (120km/75 miles round-trip) and a leisurely seafood lunch. The best option is to hire a car with a driver (making sure to agree a fixed price beforehand).

Barra da Tijuca

Barra da Tijuca is the first of Rio's western beaches that are strung along Avenida das Américas, part of the BR-101 coastal highway. Running parallel to the beachfront in Barra is Avenue Sernambetiba. Surfing schools, with boards for hire, can be found at regular intervals along its length. Away from the beach are modern apartment blocks, nightclubs, multi-screen cinemas and enormous shopping malls, giving it the nickname of Mini Miami. The sands of Barra are busiest at the eastern end. A stretch known as Praia do Pepê is the most fashionable part of the beach. A snack stand of the same name honours a local man, Pepê, a world class hang-glider and surfer who was killed in 1991 during a competition.

Grumari

The lovely little beach of Grumari is a highlight on this stretch of coast. Dense Atlantic forest stretches right to the edge of the sands, forming part of an environmental protection zone. There are only a few kiosks here and parking is limited. At the eastern end, behind some rocks, is the tiny beach of Abricó, one of few nudist beaches in Rio.

Guaratiba

Wild *restinga* (rare coastal trees and shrubs) stretches along this part of the coast. The waters are generally calm off the beach of Guaratiba. The fishing tradition here is visible in the plentiful supply of small fishing boats and some excellent seafood restaurants. The long, beautiful spit of Marambaia stretches to the west, with a series of beaches that are part of a naval base and cannot be visited.

Past Guaratiba and the naval base is the impressive **Sítio de Burle Marx,** once home of the landscape designer Roberto Burle Marx.

Sítio de Burle Marx
✉ Estrada Roberto Burle Marx 2019 ☎ (21) 2410 1412 🕓 Tue–Sat 9:30–1:30; visits only by prearranged guided tour 💵 Inexpensive

Museu Casa do Pontal

This museum, created in 1950, is a real gem. It houses one of the most important collections of folk art in Brazil, and includes 5,000 exhibits, from wood carvings to decorated figures made of dough and straw, many of them touching in their simplicity. The pieces are divided by theme, so one room may be dedicated to work depicting religious scenes, another rituals and celebrations. There is even a section on erotic art (adults only permitted). One of the highlights is the Carnaval Parade, complete with animated performers and audience.

www.museucasadopontal.com.br

✉ Estrada do Pontal 3295, Recreio dos Bandeirantes ☎ (21) 2490 3278;
🕐 Tue–Sun 9:30–5 ✋ Moderate

Prainha

Prainha (Little Beach) is a compact area of sand backed by densely forested hills and dotted with enormous boulders sculpted by the sea. This is one of Rio's best surfing beaches where locals can be seen trying to catch a wave almost every day of the week. There are a few well-used kiosks here, and limited car parking. Surf Bus (www.surfbus.com.br) operates a surf school, as well as a daily shuttle service from Rio to this and other surfing beaches.

Recreio dos Bandeirantes

The quiet beach and neighbourhood of Recreio dos Bandeirantes are 45km (28 miles) from the city centre. Many of the roads here are unpaved and, unlike nearby Barra, there are no skyscrapers or modern developments. The long beach, pounded by powerful waves, begins as an extension at the western end of sprawling Barra da Tijuca and ends at Pontal Rock. The sands here are well used by local families, as well as by volleyball players and surfers.

Inland is the reserve of **Parque Ecológico Chico Mendes,** a 40ha (100-acre) conservation area named after enrionmentalist and union leader Chico Mendes, who fought hard to save the Amazon rainforest and was tragically murdered in 1988. Visitors can see a large number of bromeliads, birds and animals such as turtles and three-fingered sloths, as well as baby alligators in a designated nursery area. There are a number of trails, picnic areas and benches throughout the park, including a children's playground, and parts of the landscape are given over to rare *restinga* (flooded salt marshes).

Parque Ecológico Chico Mendes

✉ Avenida Jarbas de Carvalho

☎ (21) 2437 6400 🕐 Tue–Sun 8–5

👆 Free

TERESÓPOLIS

Dona Teresa, Dom Pedro II's wife, fell in love with the natural beauty of this region in Brazil's highlands and the "City of Teresa" is named in tribute to her. At 910m (2,985ft) above sea level,its cool mountain climate offered welcome relief from Rio. In 1908, a new rail connection from Rio, 87km (54 miles) away, brought an influx of tourists. The snaking mountain road, completed in 1959, saw a second boom. Today, celebrities and bankers live it up in plush holiday chalets, or rough it in log cabins and working farms.

While Petrópolis (➤ 170–171), with its palaces and historic houses, resonates with the grand old days of the empire, modern Teresópolis is a popular base for hiking trips and rock climbing in dramatic mountains covered in forest and highland scrub, and cut through by pretty rivers and waterfalls, which form the **Parque Nacional Serra dos Órgãos.** European explorers named the Organ Pipe mountains after the church organ pipes they were so familiar with at home. There is a visitor centre near the park entrance, with information on the many trails available.

One of the most scenic runs for 42km (26 miles) between Teresópolis and Petrópolis, and takes three to four days. As well as shorter trails of just an hour or two, there are longer trails that wind around the park's magnificent granite peaks. There are also opportunities for canyoning and rappelling. Climbs include the 1,700m (5,577ft) Dedo de Deus (Finger of God), the 1,920m (6,300ft) Nariz do Frade (Monk's Nose) and the 2,050m (6,725ft) Agulha do Diabo (Devil's Needle).

The park boasts a rich biodiversity of bird and animal life, including armadillos and monkeys such as the endangered *muriqui* (woolly spider monkey), and has a well-developed infrastructure, including a campsite and picnic areas. The clear water of the park's biggest river, the Soberbo, which tumbles into scenic waterfalls and still pools, offers bathing opportunities.

Parque Nacional Serra dos Órgãos

✉ Avenida Rotarian s/n ☎ (21) 2152 1100; www.icmbio.gov.br/parnaso
🕐 Tue–Sun 8–5 ✋ Moderate ❓ Entrance to camping and mountain areas (Tue–Sun 6am–10pm) only with advance-purchase tickets

HOTELS

ANGRA DOS REIS
Hotel Vila Gale Eco Resort de Angra ($$$)

This 300-room resort hotel stands in the grounds of an old estate with some of the original buildings laid out around attractive lagoon-like pools. With facilities such as kids' clubs and playgrounds, it is great for families, but equally suitable for couples seeking a romantic break and even for groups.

✉ Estrada Vereador Benedito Adelino 841 ☎ (24) 33 79 28 00; www.vilagale.pt

BÚZIOS
Pousada Vila Pitanga ($)

This charming, small hotel is a real bargain. In a good location in the centre of the peninsula, it's just a 10-minute walk from the main town and close to Ferradura beach. The spacious bedrooms with high ceilings all have small fridges stocked with soft drinks and beers, while the pool, hammocks and garden are good places to relax. The whole hotel is very clean, and the owner, Denise, cannot do enough for her guests.

✉ Rua G4 6, Praia de Ferradura ☎ (22) 2623 7721; www.vilapitangabuzios.com.br

ILHA GRANDE
Pousada Naturalia ($–$$)

Set back from the beach and surrounded by vegetation, this hotel is a pleasant 10-minute walk from "town". The balconies with hammocks are a joy. Environmentally, the place loses points for its air-conditioning, but the hot water is solar powered, and there are no televisions.

✉ Praia do Abraão ☎ (24) 3361 9583, (24) 3361 9584 or (24) 9825 1316; www.pousadanaturalia.net

PARATY
Pousada Bambu Bamboo ($$$)

This relaxing and romantic hotel on the edge of the historic centre has a lovely deck overlooking the river – particularly enjoyable on a candlelit evening. The pool is a reasonable size for Paraty and there is even a spa, as well as a library and TV room with DVDs. The buffet breakfast is excellent and the staff really seem to care about their guests. Loft rooms can feel rather cramped; the suites are better value.

✉ Rua Glauber Rocha 9, Portal das Artes ☎ (24) 3371 8629;
www.bambubamboo.com

Pousada Guaraná ($)

The American/Brazilian hosts of this friendly little bed-and-breakfast are
a mine of information and can't seem to do enough for their guests.
The cats, DVD library and hammocks all make you feel right at home.
It's in a quiet location just on the edge of town, surrounded by dense
gardens, and is about a 20-minute walk from the centre, but guests
can borrow bikes at no charge.

✉ Rua 5 13, Portal de Parati ☎ (24) 3371 6362; www.pousadaguarana.com.br

PÉTROPOLIS
Hotel Solar do Império ($$)

This hotel is in an excellent location near the centre of the city, although
some of the rooms facing the street can be noisy. It's housed in an
historic, neoclassical mansion built in 1875 by a coffee baron, and there
are lush gardens and a very decent restaurant. The staff are both
friendly and helpful and the breakfasts very good.

✉ Avenida Koeler 376 ☎ (24) 2103 3000; www.solardoimperio.com.br

TERESÓPOLIS
Pousada Rosa dos Ventos ($$)

Surrounded by forest, this charming alpine-style lodge next to a lake, is
the perfect base from which to explore the surrounding countryside, on
foot or on horseback. It's smoothly run, with a friendly owner, the food
(and cocktails) are of a very high standard, and there's a shared games
room and lounge.

✉ Estrada Teresópolis-Friburgo (RJ 130) Km 23 ☎ (21) 2644 9900;
www.rosadosventos.com.br

RESTAURANTS

BARRA DA TIJUCA
Barraca do Pepê ($)

Tuck into a healthy sandwich, fresh juice or a hamburger at this beach
bar that has long been a surfer's hang-out. Named after the professional
hang-glider and surfer Paulo Carneior Lopes, otherwise known as Pepê,

who died in a hang-gliding accident in 1991, this simple spot attracts some of the most famous and beautiful people in the whole of Rio.

✉ Avenida do Pepê, Quiosque 11 ☎ (21) 2433 140; www.pepe.com.br

🕓 Daily 8–8

BÚZIOS
Chez Michou ($–$$)

This crêperie and meeting place is something of a local legend. Locals and visitors gather after sunset for the excellent crêpes and very good cocktails. Savoury and sweet crêpes of all kinds are on the menu, and you can even make your own. The loud music and large TV tuned to the sports channel may not appeal to everyone.

✉ Rua das Pedras 90 ☎ (22) 2623 2169; www.chezmichou.com.br

🕓 Mon–Wed 5:30pm–1am, Thu–Sun noon–2am

GRUMARI
Restaurante Point de Grumari ($$)

One of greater Rio's most delightful lunch spots, this beachfront restaurant, with its enchanting atmosphere, specializes in locally caught seafood and fish. Eat al-fresco on the rustic terrace overlooking the ocean while you listen to the daily live music. Booking is advised. Note that the restaurant is not open for dinner.

✉ Estrada do Grumari 710 ☎ (21) 2410 1434 🕓 Daily 11:30–6:30

PARATY
Casa do Fogo ($$$)

Seafood and Brazilian cuisine, along with some European dishes, are served up in this intimate bistro with rustic decor. There is live music most nights, from chorinho to bossa nova, and a good selection of wines and *cachaças*. The food isn't cheap, but of a consistently good quality that continues to attract discerning diners.

✉ Rua Comendador José Luiz 390 ☎ (24) 8127 1644; www.casadofogo.com

🕓 Daily 1–1

Grao de Terra ($)

This vegetarian restaurant serves delicious food that will also appeal to carnivores. Fresh organic salads and two daily specials that might include vegetarian lasagne or quiche, as well as over a hundred combinations of juices, are on the menu. Credit cards are not accepted.

✉ Avenida Roberto Silveira 328, Loja No. 9 ☎ (24) 3371 8626 ⏰ Tue–Sat 9–9

PETRÓPOLIS
Pousada da Alcobaça ($$$)

Fresh local cuisine, using produce from a nearby orchard and vegetable garden, is served in this delightful restaurant that is one of the best in the region. Choose from dishes such as duck with plums, freshly caught trout and locally prepared sausages. Booking advised.

✉ Rua Agostinho Goulão 298 ☎ (24) 2221 1240; www.pousadadaalcobaca.com.br
⏰ Daily 12–10

SHOPPING

BARRA DA TIJUCA
Barra Shopping

The sprawling, 30-year-old shopping mall in Barra da Tijuca is one of the largest in South America. With more than 500 stores, it's a shopper's paradise and also boasts restaurants, cinemas, a bowling alley and even a medical centre. As if that weren't enough, a monorail has been added to transport visitors to the various car parks.

✉ Avenida das Américas 4666 ☎ (21) 4403 4131; www.barrashopping.com.br
⏰ Shops: Mon–Sat 10–10, Sun 1–9; restaurants: Mon–Sun 10am–11pm

PARATY
Empório da Cachaça

This *cachaça* emporium stocks several hundred kinds of Brazil's national spirit. Pop in for an education in "pinga", as *cachaça* is known, or to buy a bottle to enjoy on your trip or to take home as a souvenir.

✉ Rua Doutor Samuel Costa 22 ☎ (24) 3371 7519 ⏰ Daily 11–11

ENTERTAINMENT

ANGRA DOS REIS
Mambo Jungle Adventures

This well-organized agency offers a wide range of on- and offshore activities around Angra dos Reis. Onshore activities range from horse riding, cycling and trekking to tennis and golf. Offshore tours include catamaran boat trips, diving sessions, fishing, rafting, surfing, kayaking and banana boating. You can even take to the air on a panoramic flight by helicopter or light aircraft.

✉ BR-101 Km 513, Marina Porto Frade ☎ (21) 24 3369 2371; www.mambojungle.com.br ✋ Expensive

PARATY
Angatu

This upmarket agency, with a commitment to the environment, offers Brazilians and discerning overseas visitors small tailor-made tours (many by boat).

☎ (11) 3872 0945; www.angatu.com 🕐 Mon–Sat 9–6 ✋ Expensive

Paraty Adventure

Offering true eco tours, including fascinating cultural tours, mountain biking, ocean kayaking, diving and fishing, as well as the more standard boat trips around the bay and visits to Trinidade. Consider one of the longer tours (itineraries can be arranged for up to seven days), which take you to some unspoiled beaches and other spots along the coast.

✉ Avenida Roberto Silveira 80 ☎ (24) 3371 6135; www.paratyadventure.com 🕐 Daily 8am–10pm ✋ Expensive

Teatro Espaço

This puppet theatre puts on highly acclaimed shows that use mostly mime, so no knowledge of Portuguese is needed to understand them. Purchase tickets in advance from the box office.

✉ Rua Dona Geralda 327 ☎ (24) 3371 1575; www.ecparaty.org.br 🕐 Wed, Sat 9pm ✋ Expensive

PETRÓPOLIS
Rio Hiking

This Rio-based company has many years' experience offering day trips to the city of Petrópolis, including walks in the nearby national park. It also organizes day trips to Grumari, which include cultural visits, as well as hiking, and single- and two-day trips to Ilha Grande with snorkelling opportunities. Check details on the website.

☎ (21) 2552 9204 or (21) 9721 0594; www.riohiking.com.br ✋ Expensive

Sight locator index

This index relates to the maps on the cover. We have given map references to the main sights in the book. Some sights may not be plotted on the maps.

Arpoador **19M**

Avenida Atlântica **19L–22J**

Bondinho **9C–7D**

Casa de Rui Barbosa **20G**

Catedral Metropolitana **9C**

Copacabana Palace **21J**

Cristo Redentor **16G**

Estádio do Maracanã **1C**

Forte de Copacabana **19M**

Forte Duque de Caxias **23J**

Garota de Ipanema **17M**

Igreja e Mosteiro de São Bento **9A**

Igreja Nossa Senhora do Monte do Carmo **9B**

Igreja da Ordem Terceira do Carmo **9B**

Ilha Fiscal **11A**

Instituto Moreira Salles **13L (off map)**

Jardim Botânico **14J**

Jóquei Clube Brasileiro **14K**

Lapa **9D**

Leblon **14L**

Marina da Glória **10E**

Mirante do Leblon **13M (off map)**

Morro Dois Irmãos **13M (off map)**

Morro do Leme **23J**

Museu Amsterdam Sauer **16L**

Museu de Arte Moderno **10D**

Museu do Bonde **8E**

Museu Casa de Benjamin Constant **7E**

Museu da Chácara do Céu **8D**

Museu H. Stern **16M**

Museu Histórico da Cidade **13L (off map)**

Museu Histórico Nacional **10C**

Museu do Índio **19G**

Museu Nacional **2B**

Museu Nacional de Belas Artes **9C**

Museu da República **9F**

Museu Villa-Lobos **19G**

Pão de Açúcar **24G**

Parque da Catacumba **17K**

Parque da Cidade **13L (off map)**

Parque Nacional da Tijuca **13H**

Parque das Ruínas **8D**

Planetário **13L**

Praça General Osório **18M**

Praça Nossa Senhora da Paz **17M**

Praça XV **10B**

Praia de Copacabana **19M–21J**

Praia do Ipanema **16M–18M**

Praia do Leblon **14M**

Praia do Leme **22J**

Rocinha **13L (off map)**

Santa Teresa, Largo dos Guimarães **7D**

São Conrado **13L (off map)**

Theatro Municipal **9C**

Index

accommodation *see* hotels
air travel 26–27
Angra dos Reis 155, 178, 181–182
antiques market 67
Arco do Teles 49, 84, 85
Arcos da Lapa 96
Armação de Búzios 157
Army History Museum 115
Arpoador 68, 136
Atlantic rainforest *see* Mata Atlântica
ATMs 30
Avenida Atlântica 114

Bahia 13
Baixo Bebê 70, 142
ballet 75
Banda de Ipanema 10
banks 30, 32
Barra de Guaratiba 62
Barra da Tijuca 58, 62, 172, 179–180, 181
bars 10, 92, 102, 112, 124, 151
beaches 10, 50–53, 62–63, 116, 118–119, 136, 142, 145, 155, 156, 160, 162, 164
beaches of the West Zone 172–175
beachwear 66, 150
beer 65
boat trips 70, 105, 157, 182
bondinho 70, 94, 97
Bom Retiro 47, 108
book fair 25
bookshops 102, 150
bossa nova 136, 151
Botafogo 104
Botanic Gardens 40–41, 59, 72, 130–131
botecos 10
botequims 10, 92
Burle Marx, Roberto 42, 72, 73, 98, 114, 126, 173
buses 27, 28
Búzios 156–159, 178, 180
Búzios Atlantic Forest Ecological Institute 158, 159

cable car 19, 44–45, 70
cachaça 15, 64, 65, 66, 151
Caminho do Ouro 166, 168
Caminho dos Pescadores 118
Capela de Nossa Senhora da Aparedica 37

Capela de São João 128
Capela Mayrink 47, 108
car rental 29
Cara de Cão 44
Carnaval 10, 11, 24, 74
Casa do Barão de Mauá 171
Casa da Cultura 168
Casa da Ipiranga 171
Casa Navio 96
Casa de Rui Barbosa 104
Casa de Santos Dumont 171
Cascata Diamantina 47
Cascatinha do Taunay 47, 108
Castelo Valentim 96
Catacombs Park 72, 127
Catedral Metropolitana 80
Catedral de São Pedro de Alcântara 171
Centro and São Cristóvão 79–92
Centro Cultural Banco do Brasil 16, 85, 90, 92
Centro Cultural Carioca 92
Centro Histórico *see* Centro and São Cristóvão
Chafariz da Pirâmide 85
Chafariz das Saracuras 142
Charitas 164
children's entertainment 70–71
Christ the Redeemer 18, 36–37, 68, 71
churrascarias 14, 17
Cine Gallery 55
Cine Santa Teresa 55
City History Musuem 128
City Park 128
classical music concerts 75
climate and seasons 22
climbing 58, 112, 177
coconut water 14, 64
coffee 14, 64
cog railway 36, 71
Contemporary Art Museum (MAC) 165
Copacabana 50–51, 113, 114–115, 118–119
Copacabana and Urca 113–124
Copacabana Palace 114–115, 124
Corcovado 36
Costa Verde 154, 166
Cove of Kings 155
crafts 67
credit and debit cards 30
crime 32

Cristo Redentor 18, 36–37, 68, 71
cruise ships 27, 105
cultural centres 85, 90, 92, 126, 168
currency 30
cycling 29, 58

Dedo de Deus 177
dental treatment 23, 32
Devil's Beach 136
diving and snorkelling 112, 155, 156, 157
doctors 32
drinking water 32
drive
Tijuca Forest 108–109
driving 22, 28–29
drugs, prescription 32

eco tours 182
electricity 31
embassies and consulates 31
emergency telephone numbers 31
entertainment
Centro and São Cristóvão 92
Copacabana and Urca 124
excursions 181–182
Guanabara Bay to Tijuca Forest 112
Ipanema 151
Lagoa 134
Santa Teresa and Lapa 102
Escadaria Selarón 93, 94–95
Escolas de Samba 10
essential experiences 16–19
Estádio do Maracanã 16, 38–39
excursions 152–182

farmer's market 138
Fashion Mall 145
favelas 11, 71, 140, 145
festivals and events 24–25
film festivals 24, 25
Finger of God 177
Fishermen's Walk 118
flight times 27
flip-flops 67
Floresta da Tijuca 108–109
food and drink 12–15, 60–61, 64–65
football 16, 38–39, 58
Football, Museum of 39

football shirts 67
foreign exchange 30
Fortaleza de Santa Cruz da
  Barra 165
Forte de Copacabana 68,
  70, 115
Forte Duque da Caxias 118
Fountain of the Pyramid 85
fuel 29

gafieiras 75
Galeria de Arte Ipanema 138
Garota de Ipanema 136–137,
  139
gay and lesbian scene 25,
  139, 151
gem museums 138, 141
gemstones 67
Girl from Ipanema 136–137,
  139
glass-bottomed catamaran
  trips 157
Gold Trail 166, 168
golf 145, 159
Green Coast 154, 166
Grumari 62, 172–173
Guanabara Bay to Tijuca Forest
  103–112
Guaratiba 173
gyms, outdoor 59

hammocks 66
hang-gliding 17, 59, 112, 145
Havaianas 67
health 22, 23, 32
hiking 17–18, 59, 112,
  162–163, 176–177, 182
Hipódromo da Gávea 127
Hippie Fair 142, 150
history 11
horse-racing 25, 127
hotels
  Centro and São Cristóvão 89
  Copacabana and Urca
    120–121
  excursions 178–179
  Guanabara Bay to Tijuca
    Forest 110
  Ipanema 146–147
  Lagoa 132
  Santa Teresa and Lapa 100

iced tea 65
Igreja e Convento de Santa
  Teresa 96

Igreja e Mosteiro de São Bento
  81, 84
Igreja Nossa Senhora da
  Candelária 84
Igreja Nossa Senhora do
  Monte do Carmo 81
Igreja de Nossa Senhora do
  Rosário 169
Igreja da Ordem Terceira do
  Carmo 82
Igreja de Santa Rita 168–169
Ilha Fiscal 82
Ilha Grande 160–163, 178
Imperial Museum 170
Indian Museum 70–71, 106
Instituto Ecológico Búzios
  Mata Atlântica 158, 159
Instituto Moreira Salles (IMS)
  72, 126
insurance 22, 23
internet access 30
Ipanema 18, 52–53, 135–151
Itacoatiara 164

Jardim Botânico 40–41, 59, 72,
  130–131
Jardim Zoológico 87
Jóquei Clube Brasileiro 25,
  127
Jorge Greco 162
juice bars 14, 65

kayaking 154, 155

Lagoa 125–134
Lagoa Rodrigo de Freitas 58,
  59, 125
landscape 11
language 33
Lapa 93, 94–95
Largo dos Guimarães 54–55,
  97
Leblon 137
LGBT festival 25

Mambucaba River 155
Manguinhos 156–157
Maracanã Stadium 16, 38–39
Marina da Glória 59, 105
markets 91, 123, 138, 142
Mata Atlântica 46, 119, 140,
  158, 160, 168
medical treatment 23, 32
Meso do Imperador 47
metro 28

Metropolitan Cathedral 80
Miranda, Carmen 85
Mirante Dona Marta 47
Mirante do Leblon 68, 140
mobile phones 31
Modern Art Museum (MAM)
  42–43
money 30
Moreira Salles Institute 72,
  126
Morro dois Irmãos 140
Morro do Leme 118
Morro da Urca 44, 45
Municipal Theatre 75, 88
Museu do Açude 47
Museu Amsterdam Sauer 141
Museu de Arte
  Contemporanea (MAC) 165
Museu de Arte Moderna
  (MAM) 42–43
Museu do Bonde 95, 97
Museu Casa de Benjamin
  Constant 98
Museu Casa do Pontal 174
Museu da Chácara do Céu
  68, 97, 98
Museu H. Stern 138, 141
Museu Histórico da Cidade
  128
Museu Histórico Nacional 83
Museu Imperial 170
Museu do Índio 70–71, 106
Museu Nacional 86–87
Museu Nacional de Belas
  Artes 87
Museu da República 106–107
Museu do Universo 129
Museu Villa-Lobos 107
Museum in the Sky 98
museum/monument opening
  hours 32
music 10–11, 67, 74–75

national holidays 25
National Museum 86–87
National Museum of Fine
  Arts 87
nature reserves 158
Niterói 164–165
nudist beaches 62, 156, 173

observation domes 129
opening hours 32
opera 75
Ossos 156

Paço Imperial 48, 49
Palácio Tiradentes 48–49
Pão de Açúcar 19, 44–45, 58, 69, 116–117
para-gliding 145
Paraty (Parati) 166–169, 178–179
Parque da Catacumba 69, 72, 127
Parque da Cidade 69, 128
Parque Ecológico Chico Mendes 175
Parque do Flamengo 72
Parque Garota de Ipanema 136
Parque Nacional Serra da Bocaina 168
Parque Nacional Serra dos Órgãos 176–177
Parque Nacional da Tijuca 18, 46–47, 59, 69, 71, 72–73
Parque do Penhasco Dois Irmãos 140
Parque das Ruínas 99
passports and visas 22
Pedra da Gávea 58
personal safety 32
Petrópolis 170–171, 179, 181, 182
pharmacies 32
Pico do Papagaio 162–163
Pico da Tijua 47, 108
Pink Fleet 105
Piratininga 164
Pista Cláudio Coutinho 59, 73, 116–117
Planetário 71, 129
police 31, 32
postal services 30, 32
postos (lifeguard posts) 51, 52
Praça dos Telescópios 129
Praça General Osório 142
Praça Nossa Senhora da Paz 142
Praça XV 48–49, 85
Praia dos Amores 156
Praia de Copacabana 50–51, 62
Praia do Diablo 136
Praia da Ferradurinha 156
Praia de Geribá 156
Praia do Ipanema 52–53, 62
Praia de João Fernandes 156
Praia do Leblon 62, 142
Praia do Leme 118–119
Praia Lopes Mendes 160, 162
Praia do Pepê 62, 172

Praia Tartaruga 156
Praia Vermelha 63, 116, 117
Praia das Virgens 156
Praias de Zona Oeste 172–175
Prainha 59, 63, 174
public transport 28
puppet theatre 182

Quinta da Boa Vista 73

rafting 155
rainforest 46, 119, 140, 158, 160, 168
Recreio dos Bandeirantes 63, 175
Republic, Museum of the 106–107
Reserva Tauá 158
restaurants
    Centro and São Cristóvão 89–91
    Copacabana and Urca 121–123
    excursions 179–181
    Guanabara Bay to Tijuca Forest 110–111
    Ipanema 147–149
    Lagoa 132–134
    Santa Teresa and Lapa 101–102
Rocinha 69, 71, 145
rodizos 14

Sacred Art Museum 80
sailing 59
samba 10–11, 17, 74, 75, 102, 124
Sambódromo 10, 75
Santa Teresa 19, 54–55, 96–97
Santa Teresa and Lapa 93–102
São Conrado 17, 145
scenic flights 182
seatbelts 28
Semana Santa (Holy Week) 24
Serra do Mar 155, 166, 168
Ship House 96
shopping 32, 66–67
    Centro and São Cristóvão 91
    Copacabana and Urca 123–124
    excursions 181
    Guanabara Bay to Tijuca Forest 112
    Ipanema 150

Lagoa 134
    Santa Teresa and Lapa 102
Sítio de Burle Marx 73, 173
snack foods 60–61
snorkelling 155, 156, 157
souvenirs 66–67
speed limits 28
sports and activities 58–59
Sugarloaf Mountain 44–45, 58, 69, 116–117
sun safety 32
sunsets 136
surfing 59, 145, 162, 174

taxis 27, 28
telephones 31
Telescope Square 129
Teresópolis 176–177, 179
Theatro Municipal 75, 88
Tijuca Forest 108–109
Tijuca National Park 46–47, 71, 72–73
time differences 23
tipping 30
tourist information 23, 29
Tram Museum 95, 97
travellers' cheques 30
travelling to Rio de Janeiro 26–27
Travesso do Comércio 49, 85
Trindade 169

Universe Museum 129
Urca 113, 117

views 68–69
Vila do Abraão 163
Villa Lobos, Heitor 107
Vista Chinesa 47

walking 59
walks
    Centro Histórico 84–85
    Ipanema 138–139
    Jardim Botânico 130–131
    Pão de Açúcar 116–117
    Santa Teresa 96–97
websites 23
windsurfing 157
wines 64

yoga 59

zoo 87

Street Index

1 de Março, Rua **B9**
2 de Dezembro **F9**
5 de Julio **K19**

Aarao Reis, Rua **E7**
A Belo **E8**
A Bueno **H20**
Acacias, Rua das **K13**
Achotegui **L14**
A Coutinho **C7**
Adalberto Ferreira **L14**
Afonso Pena **D3**
Afranio de Melo Franco,
Av **L15**
Aguiar **E2**
Aires de Saldanha **L19**
Aiuru **H17**
A Lage, Rua **A7**
Alameda Cochrane,
Rua **E1**
Alberto **H17**
Alexandre Mackenzie **B8**
Alfândega, Rua da **B8**
Alfonso Cavalcanti,
Rua **C5**
Alfredo Chaves **G18**
Alfredo Duarte **H16**
Alm Baltasar **C3**
Almirante Alexandrino,
Rua **E8**
Almirante Barroso,
Av **C9**
Almirante Guilhem **L15**
Almirante Silvio de
Noronha, Avenida
D11
Alvaro Ramos **H20**
Alverne **B5**
Alzira Brandao **E2**
Ambire Cavalcanti **E5**
America, Av da **B6**
Americo Rangel **A8**
Andre Cavalcanti **D8**
Anibal Benevolo **C6**
Anibal de Mendonça
M16
Anita Garibaldi **J19**
Antunes Maciel **C3**
Aperana **M13**
Aprazivel **E8**
Aranha **L13**
Araucaria **H16**
Araujo Pena **E3**
Araujos, Rua dos **F2**
Arce **B9**
Aristides Lobo, Rua **D4**
Arnaldo Quintela, Rua
H20
Artur Araipe, Rua **K13**
Assemleia, Rua **C9**
Ataulfo de Paiva, Av
M14
Atlântica, Avenida **J22**
Augusto Severo, Av **E9**

Aurea **E7**
Aurelinano Portugal **E3**
Azevedo **D5**
Azevedo Lima **E5**

Barão da Torre **L15**
Barão de Iguatemi,
Rua **D3**
Barão de Ipanema **K19**
Barão de Itapagipe,
Rua **E3**
Barão de Jaguaripe **L16**
Barão de Mesquita,
Rua **D2**
Barão de Petropolis,
Rua **F5**
Barao de São Felix **B7**
Barão de Uba **E4**
Barão Sertorio **E4**
Barata Ribeiro, Rua **J20**
Bario Gamboa, Rua
da **B6**
Barros **B6**
Barros **E4**
Barroso **H22**
Barroso, Rua do **B7**
Bartolomeu de Gusmao,
Av **C1**
Bartolomeu Mitre,
Av **K14**
Bartolomeu Portela **G21**
Beira Mar, Avenida **D9**
Belford Roxo **J21**
Benjamin Batista **H15**
Benjamin Constant **E8**
Bento Lisboa, Rua **F9**
Bento Ribeiro, Rua **B7**
Bernadotte **L14**
Bernardes **F9**
Bernardino dos Santos
E8
B Hipolito, Rua **C6**
Bispo, Rua do **E4**
Boamorte, Rua **C4**
Bogari **H17**
Bolivar, Rua **L19**
Bom Pastor, Rua **F1**
Borges de Medeiros,
Avenida **J16**
Brasil, Avenida **A4**
Brito **H20**
Buarque do Macedo **F9**
Buenos Aires, Rua
de **C8**
Bulhoes Carvalho,
Rua **L18**
Burie **H18**

C, Rua **K17**
Caio Melo **H16**
Camerino, Rua **B8**
Campo Se São Cristóvão
A3
Campos da Paz **E4**

Campos Sales **D3**
Candido Oliveira, Rua **F5**
Caning **M18**
Cantuaria **G23**
Capitan Salomao **H18**
Cardoso Marinho **B6**
Carioca, Rua da **C8**
Carlos de Vasconcelos
E1
Carlos Gois **L14**
Carlos Gomes **B5**
Carlos Peixoto **H21**
Carmela Dufra **E2**
Carmo Neto **C6**
Carolina Reydner **D6**
Caruso **D4**
Casurina **H18**
Catete, Rua do **E9**
Catumbi, Rua do **D6**
Caturama, Rua **F5**
Ceasra **C3**
Cecilia **E5**
Celso **H15**
Cesar Andrade **L14**
Cesario Alvim **G18**
Churchill, Av **C10**
Cidade de Lima, Avenida
A5
Citiso **E4**
C Martins **E5**
Codajas **L13**
Coelho E Castro **A8**
Com C Farias **D3**
Com Pires **B4**
Conde de Bonfim,
Rua **E1**
Conde de Iraja, Rua **G18**
Cons Zacarias **A7**
Constante Ramos,
Rua **K19**
Constituicao, Rua de **C8**
Coqueiros, Rua dos **D7**
Corcovado **J14**
Cordeiro da Gracia **A5**
Correia **K19**
Correia Dutra **F9**
Costa Ferraz **E5**
Cruzeiro **E6**
Cruzeiro Sul **F8**
C Sampaio, Rua **D7**
Cunha Barbosa **A7**
Cupertino Durao **M14**

David Campista **G18**
Decio Vilares **J19**
De Freitas **D9**
Delfim Moreira, Avenida
M14
Delgado de Carvalho **E3**
Deputade Soares
Filho **D1**
Dias de Barros **D8**
Dias de Rocha **K19**
Dias Ferreira, Rua **M13**

Dr Agra, Rua **E6**
Dr Araujo **D4**
Dr S Leite **E7**
Dr Satamine, Rua **D3**
Dr Xavier Sigaud **H22**
Dom Gerardo, Rua **A9**
Domicio da Gama **D4**
Domingos Ferreira **K19**
Dona Mariana **G19**
Dr A Barros **E2**
Dulce **D2**
Duvivier **J21**

E, Rua **K17**
Ebroino Urugual **B6**
Eleone de Almeida,
Rua **D7**
Eliseu Visconti **E6**
Emilia Guimaraes **D6**
Eng Adel **E3**
Eng Pena Chaves **J14**
Enrico Cruz **H17**
Epitacio Pessoa, Avenida
L16
Equador, Rua **A5**
Erfurt, Rua **F8**
Escragnole Doria **F6**
Espinola **M13**
Estela **J14**
Esteves **J13**
Estrela, Rua da **E4**
Euclides da Rocha **J18**
Euclides Figueiredo **H17**
Eugenheiro Freyssinet,
Av **E4**
Evaristo da Veiga,
Rua **C9**

Fadel Fadel **L14**
Falet **F6**
Faria, Rua do **B7**
Farme de Amoedo **M17**
Faro **H15**
Felix da Cunha, Rua **E2**
Felix Pacheco **L13**
Ferreira do Viana **F9**
F Freijo **C8**
F Graca **F1**
Fialho **J14**
Fialho, Rua do **E9**
Figueira de Melo,
Rua **B3**
Figueiredo Magalhães,
Rua **J19**
F Magalhaes **J14**
Fonte da Saudade, Rua
da **J17**
Francisca de Andrade **E8**
Francisco Bicalho,
Avenida **B4**
Francisco Eugenio,
Rua **C3**
Francisco Otaviano, Rua
M18

Francisco Sa, Rua **M18**
Frassinetti **E4**
Frei Caneca, Rua **C7**
Frei Leandro **H17**
Frei Orlando **D7**
Freitas **J20**
Frolick **B3**
F Silva **C7**

G A Calogeras, Av **C9**
Gago Coutinho **F8**
Gamboa, Rua da **A6**
Garcia d'Avila **M16**
Gen Artigas **M14**
Gen B Lima **J20**
Gen Caldwell **C7**
Gen Canabarro, Rua **D2**
Gen Cardoso de Aguilar **H21**
Gen Dionisio **H18**
Gen Falcao **E6**
Gen Galvao **E6**
Gen Garzon **J15**
Gen G Monteiro **H21**
Gen Hercules Gomes, Rua **C2**
Gen Justo, Av **C10**
Gen Luis M Morais, Rua **B5**
Gen Marcelino **D2**
Gen Mariante **F7**
Gen Polidoro, Rua **H20**
Gen Rabelo **K13**
Gen R Costa **J22**
Gen Roca, Rua **E1**
Gen San Martin, Av **M14**
Gen Severiano, Rua **G21**
Gen Venancio Flores, Rua **M14**
G Guinle **G19**
Gilberto Cardoso, Rua **L14**
Glória, Rua da **D9**
Goitacazes **E9**
Golemburgo **B4**
Gomes Carneiro, Rua **M18**
Gomes Freire, Avenida **C8**
Goncalves Crespo, Rua **D3**
Gonçalves Dias **B9**
Goncalves Ledo **B8**
Gorceix de Sa **L17**
Goulart **E2**
Guaicurus **F5**
Guaoaira **E1**
Guapeni **E1**
Guim **G20**
Guimaraes **E8**
Guimaraes **G20**
Gustavo Sampaio **J22**

Haddock Lobo, Rua **D4**
Heitor Beltrao, Av **E1**
Heloisa **J14**
Henrique Dodsworth, Av **L18**
Henrique Dumont **M15**
Henrique Valdares, Av **D7**
Hermenegildo de Barros **D9**
Hilario de Gouveia **J20**
H Oswald, Rua **J19**
Humaita, Rua **H17**
Humberto de Campos, Rua **L14**

Ibiturana, Rua **C3**
Icatu **G18**
Igrejinha, Rua da **A3**
Infante de Sagres **F4**
Infante Dom Henrique, Avenida **D9**
Ingles de Souza **H14**
Inhomirim **B3**
Invalidos, Rua dos **C8**
Itaipava **H15**
Itapiru, Rua **E6**
Itiquira **L13**

Jacuma **E3**
J Alencar, Rua **D7**
Japeri **E4**
Jaqueira **F6**
Jardel Jercolis **D10**
Jardim Botânico, Rua **H15**
J Cardoso **B5**
J Carlos **H16**
Jequitiba, Rua do **K13**
Jiquiba **C3**
Joana Angelica **M17**
Joao Afonso **G18**
Joao Barros **L14**
Joao Neves de Fontoura, Rua **D10**
Joao Paulo I, Rua **D4**
Joaquim Campos Porto **J13**
Joaquim Murtinho, Rua **D8**
Joaquim Nabuco, Rua **M18**
Joaquim Palhares, Rua **D4**
Joaquim Pizarro **F3**
Joaquim Silva **D9**
Jogo da Bola, Rua do **B8**
Jorge da Silva **E7**
J Palhares, Rua **C4**
Julio Carmo **C6**
Julio de Castilhos **M19**
Junquilhos, Rua dos **F2**

Ladeira do Castro **D8**
Ladeira do Leme, Rua **J21**
Ladeira dos Tabajaras **J19**
Ladeira Santa Teresa **D9**
Lafaiete **M19**
Lapa, Rua da **D9**
Largo do Curvelo **E8**
Largo dos Guimarães **E8**
Laurindo Rabelo, Rua **D5**
Lauro Muller **H21**
Lavradio, Rua do **C8**
Leal **J22**
Leandro Martins **B8**
Leoncio Correia **L13**
L Ferraz **B3**
Lima **E3**
Lineu de Rua Paula Machado, Av **J15**
Linhares **L14**
Lira **M14**
Livamento, Rua do **A7**
Livramento, **A7**
Lopes de Sousa **C3**
Losio **F2**
Lucia, Rua da **B7**
Lucio Mendonca **D2**

Macaubas **G19**
Macedo Sobrinho **H18**
Machado Assis **F9**
Maestro Francisco Braga **J19**
Magno, Rua **E8**
M Aguinaldo, Rua **C10**
Maia de Lacerda, Rua **D5**
Major Freitas **D5**
Major Rubens Vaz **K13**
Manuel **G20**
Maracana, Av **D1**
Marco, Avenida de **C6**
Marechal Floriano, Avenida **B7**
Maria Angelica **H16**
Maria Eugenia **H17**
Maria Quiteria, Rua **M16**
Marink Velga **B9**
Mario Ribeiro **L14**
Maris Barros, Rua **D3**
Marques **G18**
Marques de Pombal, Rua **C6**
Marques de Valenca **C6**
Marques do Sapucai, Rua **C6**
Martins Pena **D3**
Martius Ferreira **G18**
Mata Machado, Rua **C1**
Matilde **F1**
Matoso, Rua do **D4**
Matriz, Rua da **G19**
M Brito, Rua **E2**

M Camara, Av **C10**
M Castro **H20**
Melo E Sousa **B4**
Melo Matos **E3**
Mem de Sa, Avenida **C7**
Mena Barreto, Rua **H19**
Meneses **D1**
Mercado **B9**
Mexico **C9**
M F Moura **G19**
Miguel Lemos, Rua **L18**
Miguel Pereira **H17**
Miguel Resende **E7**
M Lebrao **E9**
M Mascarenhas de Morais **J20**
Moncorvo Filho **C7**
Monte, Rua do **A7**
Monte Alegre **D8**
Monteiro **M13**
Morais E Silva **D2**
Morgan **H17**
Mota **D4**
M Pinto, Rua **B5**
M R Castilla **H21**
M S Uchoa, Rua **C4**

Nabuco de Freitas **B6**
Nascimento Silva **L16**
Natal **J20**
Navarro **E6**
Negreiros **B5**
Neri Pinheiro **C5**
Nestor Vitor **D3**
Nilo Pecanha, Av **C9**
Nossa Senhora de Copacabana, Avenida **K20**
N S de Fatima **D7**

Ocidental **E7**
O Fausto **H20**
Oitis, Rua dos **K13**
Oliveira **J21**
Oliveira Castro **J13**
Oliveira Rocha **H15**

Pachaco Leao, Rua **J14**
Padre L Franca **L13**
Padre Miguelino **D7**
Palmeiras, Rua das **G19**
Para **C3**
Paraiba **C3**
Paraiso, Rua do **D7**
Parreiras **M18**
Paschoal, Rua **E7**
Passagem, Rua da **G20**
Passeio, Rua do **D9**
Pasteur, Avenida **G21**
Paul Redfem **M15**
Paula Matos **D7**
Paulino Fernandes **G20**
Paulo Barreto **G20**
Paulo C Andrade **F8**

Pedro Alves **B5**
Pedro Americo, Rua **E8**
Pedro Antonio **B8**
Pedro Ernesto, Rua **A7**
Pedro Guedes **C3**
Pedro II, Av **B3**
Pepe **G20**
Pereira da Silva **F7**
Pereira de Almeida **C4**
Pereira de Siqueira **E2**
Pereira Franco, Rua **C6**
Peri **H14**
Pertence **E9**
Pimentel **E3**
Pinheiro Guimaraes,
   Rua **H18**
Pinto **E2**
Pinto, Rua do **B6**
Pio Correa **H17**
Piracinunga **F1**
Piragibe **B5**
Pocone **H17**
Porto **H17**
Portugal, Avenida **G22**
Potengi, Rua **F1**
Praça Cruz Vermelha **G22**
Praca da Republica **B8**
Praca do Flamengo **F9**
Prado Junior **D4**
Pres A Carlos, Av **C10**
Pres Barroso **C6**
Pres Castelo Branco,
   Av **C1**
Presidente Kubitschek,
   Avenida **A8**
Presidente Vargas,
   Av **B7**
Pres Wilson, Av **D10**
Princesa Isabel, Avenida
   J21
Prof A Lobo, Rua **H17**
Prof A M Teixeira **L15**
Prof A Rodrigues, Rua
   G20
Prof Eurico Rabelo,
   Rua **C1**
Prof Gabiso, Rua **D2**
Prof Gastao Bahiana **L18**
Prof Pereira Reis, Av **A5**
Prof Quintino do Vale **D4**
Prof Ribeir **L15**
Progresso **D7**
Proposito, Rua do **A7**
Prudente de Morais,
   Rua **M17**

Queiros Lima **E6**
Quimaraes **H20**
Quintas **H14**
Quitanda, Rua da **B9**

Rainha Elizabeth, Av
   M18
Rainha Guilhermina **M13**

Ramon Franco **G22**
Ramos **H15**
Ramos **L15**
Rangel **E9**
Raul Pompeia, Rua **L19**
R D Catumbi **D6**
R D Lopez **J21**
Real Grandeza, Rua **G19**
Redentor **L16**
Redentor, Estrada
   da **G13**
Rego Lopes **E2**
Relacao, Rua da **C8**
Rep de Peru, Rua **J20**
Rep do Paraguai **C9**
Republica do Chile,
   Av **C8**
Rezende, Rua do **D8**
Riachuelo, Rua **D7**
Ribeiro **H17**
Ribeiro **J14**
Rio Branco, Avenida **A9**
Rio de Janeiro, Avenida
   A4
Rita Ludolf **M13**
Rivadavia Correia,
   Rua **A6**
Rocha Faria **H14**
Rodolfo Dantas **J21**
Rodrigo Otavio, Avenida
   L14
Rodrigues Alves,
   Avenida **A5**
Roosevelt, Avenida **C10**
Rosa Saiao **B7**
R Pompeu Loureiro **K18**
R Santos **C5**
Ruo do Oriente **D7**
Russel **E9**
Russel **L14**

Sacadura Cabral, Rua **A7**
Sacopa **J17**
Sadock **L17**
Sa Ferreira, Rua **L18**
St Roman **L18**
Saldanha Marinho **C5**
Salvador Sa, Avenida **D5**
Sampaio **H17**
Sampaio Viana **E4**
San Gavito **G21**
Santa Alexandrina **E4**
Santa Amelia **D4**
Santa Clara, Rua **J18**
Santa Cristina **E8**
Santa Luzia, Rua de **C9**
Santana, Rua de **C7**
Santa Sofia **E1**
Santo Amaro **E8**
Santo Cristo, Rua **A6**
Santos **D7**
Santos **F8**
Santos Lima, Rua **A3**
São Carlos **D5**

São Claudio **D5**
São Clemente, Rua **G19**
São Cristóvão, Rua **B3**
São Francisco Xavier,
   Rua **D1**
São Joao Batista, Rua
   G19
São Jose **C9**
São Roberto **D5**
São Sebastiao **G23**
Saraiva **B9**
Sat de Brito **J15**
Sauro Sodre, Av **H21**
Sena **B5**
Senado, Rua do **C7**
Senador Pompeu,
   Rua **B6**
Sen Furtado, Rua **C3**
Senhor do Matozinhos
   D6
Senhor dos Passos **C8**
Senhora **E9**
Sen L Bittenc **H17**
Sera **B5**
Serrao **H17**
Silveira Martins **F9**
Silvio Romero **D8**
Simonsen **H15**
Siqueira **D3**
Siqueira Campos,
   Rua **J19**
S Montenegro **A7**
Soares **J17**
Soares Costa **E1**
Sobradinho **F6**
Soledade **D3**
Soltero dos Reis **C3**
Sorocaba **G19**
Sousa E Silva **A7**
Sousa Lima **L18**
S Rodrigues **D5**
Sumare, Estrada do **F3**

Tabatinguera **K16**
Tanimbo, Rua **E6**
Tavares Bastos **F8**
Taylor **D9**
Tefe, Av **A8**
Teixeira, Rua **D9**
Teixeira de Melo **M18**
Teixeira Soares, Rua **C3**
Teofilo Otoni **B8**
Timoteo da Costa **L13**
Tome de Sousa **B8**
Tonelero, Rua **J20**
Tr Falet **E6**
Triunfo **E8**
Tunel Andres Reboucas
   G17
Tunel Santa Barbara **E7**
Tv Guedes **D5**

Urbano Santos **G22**
Urquiza **L14**

Urucui **H14**
Uruguaiana, Rua **B8**

Valentim, Rua **D9**
Valparaiso **E2**
Valverde **G18**
Van Erven **D6**
Vecente Licinio **D3**
Venceslau Bras, Av **G21**
Venezuela, Avenida **A8**
Vicente **D4**
Vieira Souto, Avenida
   M16
Vila Flor **E4**
Vilela **H14**
Vinicius de Moraes,
   Rua **M17**
Visc de Carandal **J15**
Visc do Rio Branco,
   Rua **C7**
Visc Itauna **H14**
Viscente de Caravelas
   H18
Visconde Cairu, Rua
   de **D2**
Visconde de
   Albuquerque, Avenida
   M13
Visconde de Figueiredo
   E2
Visconde de Piracinunga
   C6
Visconde de Piraja,
   Rua **M16**
Visconde de Silva,
   Rua **H18**
Visconde Gavea, Rua
   da **B7**
Visconde Inhauma,
   Rua **B9**
Vista Alegre **D7**
Vitoria Regia, Rua **J17**
Vitorio Costa **H18**
Viuva Lacerda **H18**
Viveiros de Castro **J21**
Voluntarios da Patria,
   Rua **G19**
Von Martius **J14**

Washington Luis **D7**
W Dutra, Rua **B6**

Xavier da Silveira,
   Rua **L19**

Zamenhof **D5**
Zara **J14**
Zenha **E2**
Zinco **D5**

Acknowledgements

The Automobile Association would like to thank the following photographers, companies and picture libraries for their assistance in the preparation of this book.

Abbreviations for the picture credits are as follows – (t) top; (b) bottom; (c) centre; (l) left; (r) right; (AA) AA World Travel Library.

4l Cristo Redentor, Goncalo Diniz/Alamy; **4c** Carnival at the Sambódromo, AA/Y Levy; **4r** Avenida Vieira Souto, Ipanema, AA/J Love; **5l** Cable car, Pão de Açúcar Mountain, AA/J Love; **5c** Praia da Urca, AA/J Love; **5r** Niterói from Pão de Açúcar, AA/J Love; **6/7** Cristo Redentor, Goncalo Diniz/Alamy; **8/9** Ipanema, AA/J Love; **10t** Bar Gomez bodega, Santa Teresa, AA/J Love; **10b** Carnival at the Sambódromo, AA/Y Levy; **11** Praia do Ipanema, AA/J Love; **12t** Papaya for sale in Ipanema, AA/J Love; **12b** Ipanema Market, AA/J Love; **13t** Ipanema Market, AA/J Love; **13bl** Amazonian food at Espirito Santos restaurant, Santa Teresa, AA/J Love; **13br** Amazonian food at Espirito Santos restaurant, Santa Teresa, AA/J Love; **14tl** Feijoada, AA/K Blackwell; **14tr** Coconuts for sale in Praia de Copacabana, AA/J Love; **14c** Making *caipirinha* at Academia de Cachaça, Leblon, AA/J Love; **15t** Coconuts in Copacabana, AA/J Love; **15b** Coco Gelado, Praia do Ipanema, AA/J Love; **16t** Centro Cultural Banco do Brasil, AA/J Love; **16b** Estádio do Maracanã, AA/J Love; **17t** Rio Scenarium in Lapa, AA/J Love; **17bl** Porçao Restaurant in Flamengo, AA/J Love; **17br** Hang gliders on São Conrado Beach, AA/J Love; **18t** Cascatinha do Taunay in Parque Nacional da Tijuca, AA/J Love; **18b** Cristo Redentor, David Davis Photoproductions/Alamy; **19t** Praia do Ipanema, AA/J Love; **19b** Cable car in Pão de Açúcar, AA/J Love; **20/21** Carnival at the Sambódromo, AA/Y Levy; **24** Carnival at the Sambódromo, AA/Y Levy; **27** Santos Dumont Airport, AA/J Love; **34/35** Avenida Vieira Souto in Ipanema, AA/J Love; **36** Cristo Redentor, jeremy sutton-hibbert/Alamy; **37** Pão de Açúcar from Corcovado Mountain, AA/J Love; **38** Estádio do Maracanã, AA/J Love; **39** Estádio do Maracanã, AA/J Love; **40** Cómoro Frei Lendro in Jardim Botânico, AA/J Love; **41t** Orchids in Jardim Botânico, AA/J Love; **41b** Imperial Palms in Jardim Botânico, AA/J Love; **42** Museu de Arte Moderna, AA/J Love; **43** *Semente* by Kaká Versiani, 2009, Museu de Arte Moderna, AA/J Love; **44** Pão de Açúcar, AA/J Love; **45** Cable Car in Pão de Açúcar, AA/J Love; **46** Parque Nacional da Tijuca, AA/J Love; **47** Parque Nacional da Tijuca, AA/J Love; **48** Marechel Osorio Statue in Praça XV Novembro, AA/J Love; **49** Praça XV Novembro, AA/J Love; **50** Praia de Copacabana, AA/J Love; **51** Praia de Copacabana from Pão de Açúcar, AA/J Love; **52** Praia do Ipanema, AA/J Love; **53** Praia do Ipanema, AA/J Love; **54** Rua Moinho Allegre in Santa Teresa, AA/J Love; **55** Tram at Largo dos Guimarães, Santa Teresa, AA/J Love; **56/57** Cable car, Pão de Açúcar, AA/J Love; **58** Parque Nacional da Tijuca, AA/J Love; **59** Praia de Copacabana, AA/J Love; **60** Confeitaria Colombo, Forte de Copacabana, AA/J Love; **61** Espirito Santa Restaurant in Santa Teresa, AA/J Love; **63** Avenida Atlântica in Copacabana, AA/J Love; **64** Praia de Copacabana, AA/K Blackwell; **65** Bar Veloso in Leblon, AA/J Love; **66** O Sol shop in Jardim Botânico, AA/J Love; **67** Havaianas for sale, AA/K Blackwell; **68/69** Parque Nacional da Tijuca, AA/J Love; **70** Bondinho in Santa Teresa, AA/J Love; **71** Planetário in Gávea, AA/J Love; **72** Fundação Eva Klabin in Lagoa, AA/J Love; **73** Jardim Botânico, AA/J Love; **74** Samba in Semente, Lapa, AA/J Love; **76/77** Praia de Urca, AA/J Love; **79** Patio dos Canhoes in the Museum Historico Nacional, AA/J Love; **80t** Catedral Metropolitana, AA/J Love; **80b** Catedral Metropolitana, AA/J Love; **81** Igreja da NS do Monte do Carmo, AA/J Love; **82/83** Ilha Fiscal, AA/J Love; **83t** Museo Histórico Nacional, AA/J Love; **84** Travessa do Comércio, AA/J Love; **85** Travessa do Ouvidor, AA/J Love; **86** Museo Nacional de Belas Artes, Barbara Haynor/Photolibrary; **87** Sculpture gallery, Museu Nacional de Belas Artes, AA/J Love; **88** Teatro Municipal, AA/J Love; **93** Escadaria Selarón, AA/J Love; **94** Convento de Santa Teresa, AA/J Love; **95** Nightlife in Lapa, AA/J Love; **96** Museu da Chácara do Céu, AA/J Love; **97** Largo dos Guimarães, AA/J Love; **98** Casa de Benjamin Constant, AA/J Love; **99** Parque das Ruínas, AA/J Love; **103** Casa de Rui Barbosa, AA/J Love; **104/105** Marina da Glória, AA/J Love; **106** Museo do Índio, AA/J Love; **107** Palácio do Catete, AA/J Love; 109 Cascatinha do Taunay in the Floresta de Tijuca, AA/J Love; **113** Morro da Urca from Praia Botafogo, AA/J Love; **114** Copacabana Palace, AA/J Love; **115** Avenida Atlântica, AA/J Love; **116** Urca, AA/J Love; **117** Praia de Urca, AA/J Love; **119** Praia do Leme, AA/J Love; **125** Jóquei Clube and Lagoa Rodrigo de Freitas, AA/J Love; **126** Jóquei Clube from Corcovado, AA/J Love; **127** Parque da Catacumba, AA/J Love; **128** Parque da Cidade, AA/J Love; **129** Planetário, AA/J Love; **131** Jardim Botânico, AA/J Love; **135** Avenida Vieira Souto, AA/J Love; **136/137** Ponta do Arpoador, AA/J Love; **139** Avenida Vieira Souto, AA/J Love; **140/141** Ipanema from Mirante do Leblon, AA/J Love; **142/143** Praia do Leblon, AA/J Love; **144** Rocinha, AA/J Love; **152/153** Niterói from Pão de Açúcar, AA/J Love; **155** Angra dos Reis, AA/J Love; **156** Statue of Brigitte Bardot in Búzios, AA/J Love; **157** Praia dos Ossos in Búzios, AA/J Love; **158/159** Búzios, AA/J Love; **161** Ilha Grande, AA/J Love; **162/163** Praia Lopes Mendes on Ilha Grande, AA/J Love; **164** Museu de Arte Contemporanea in Niterói, AA/J Love; **165** Praia de Itacoatiara, AA/J Love; **166/167** Paraty, AA/J Love; **168** Igreja de Nossa Senhora das Dores in Paraty, AA/J Love; **169** Igreja de Santa Rita in Paraty, AA/J Love; **170** Avenue Koeler in Petrópolis, AA/J Love; **171** Catedral de São Pedro de Alcântara, AA/J Love; **172** Barra da Tijuca, AA/J Love; **173** Sítio de Burle Marx, AA/J Love; **174** Sítio de Burle Marx, AA/J Love; **175** Praia Recreio dos Bandeirantes, AA/J Love; **176/177** Dedo de Deus Peak in the Parque Nacional Serra dos Órgãos, AA/J Love.

Every effort has been made to trace the copyright holders, and we apologise in advance for any unintentional omissions or errors. We would be pleased to apply any corrections in a following edition of this publication.